SEW
VINTAGE

SEW VINTAGE

*New Creations
from
Found Fabrics*

JENNIE ARCHER ATWOOD

The Taunton Press

Cover Designer: Carol Singer
Interior Designer: Marisa Gentile
Layout Artists: Marisa Gentile, Lori Wendin
Photographers: Jack Deutsch, Sloan Howard, Randy O'Rourke
Illustrator: Christine Erikson

Text © 2002 by Jennie Archer Atwood
Photographs © 2002 by Jack Deutsch: pp. ii, v, vi-ix, 2, 5-14, 15-17,
20, 23-34, 37-44, 46-47, 49 (top), 51, 52, 53 (bottom), 55-59, 60
(top), 62 (bottom), 63 (top), 64, 65 (bottom), 66 (top and left), 67
(bottom), 68-72, 73 (left), 74, 77 (bottom), 78-83, 86, 87 (bottom,
left, and right), 89-91, 92 (bottom left and bottom right), 93-98, 99
(botttom right), 100-108, 109 (bottom), 111-113, 115-128, 130;
Sloan Howard: pp. 19, 21, 35, 45, 49 (bottom), 50, 53 (top), 61
(bottom), 62 (top), 63 (bottom) 65 (top), 66 (right), 67 (top and
center), 73 (top and right), 75, 76, 77 (top), 84, 87 (top left and
center left), 92 (top left and top right), 99 (top left, top right, and
bottom left), 109 (top left and top right), 114, 129, 131; Randy
O'Rourke: pp. 4, 22, 36, 54, 88, 110
Illustrations © 2002 by The Taunton Press, Inc.

The Taunton Press, Inc., 63 South Main Street, PO Box 5506,
Newtown, CT 06470-5506
e-mail: tp@taunton.com

Distributed by Publishers Group West

Library of Congress Cataloging-in-Publication Data
Atwood, Jennie Archer.
    Sew vintage : new life for vintage cloth / Jennie Archer Atwood.
        p.   cm.
    Includes index.
    ISBN 1-56158-630-7
    1. Sewing. 2. Textile crafts. 3. Recycling (Waste, etc.). I. Title.
TT715.A89   2002
646'.11—dc21   2001040981

Printed in Singapore
10 9 8 7 6 5 4 3 2 1

*To my mother,
Patricia Archer,
whose love and
patience nurtured
my love of
sewing, and to
my father,
Don Archer, who
always believed
in me.*

ACKNOWLEDGMENTS

Writing a book has taken me on a journey like no other I have experienced. The Taunton Press has been my travel agency negotiating new territory, and I am thankful for all their help. Acquisitions Editor Jolynn Gower assured me that words are just an expression of ideas and my ideas could be corralled, and Acquisitions Editor Carol Spier helped bring this to fruition. Assistant editor Sarah Coe was my travel agent, organizing and directing the trip. The process photo shoot, familiar to me as speaking a foreign language, was successfully completed with the skills of Sarah and photographer Sloan Howard. With the expertise of photographer Jack Deutsch, illustrator Christine Erikson, book designer Marisa Gentile, and copy editor Gilda Caserta, my book-writing journey arrived at its final destination.

My friend and sewing mentor, Linda Lee, urged me to write this book, encouraging me to explore the creative side of my character. She has provided teaching opportunities to experiment with my skills, and I thank her for her support.

When I reflect on the journey of writing this book, I realize the seeds were planted as a child. My mother's love of sewing, in combination with her technical and creative skills, showed me by example how creative passion can enrich our lives. As a mother myself, I marvel at the time she took and the patience she showed in teaching me to sew and to share her passion today. Thank you, Mom.

My sister, Donna Faye, joined me in this book-writing journey, and I am thankful for her enthusiasm and assistance along the way. She sent me countless care packages of vintage textiles, buttons, and beads, and I sent her beading projects, which she generously completed. Her editorial support was invaluable and with her journalistic expertise, I was able to express myself in a new way: with organization and proper grammar.

To my children, Allie, Stephanie, and Erin, thank you for your patience and tolerance over the duration of this journey, and for reminding me that with a P.M.A. (positive mental attitude) each day can be a little vacation.

And finally, a special thanks to my husband, Mike, who has always shown patience and humor in helping me negotiate map reading, whether on the big journey of life or the detours like writing a book.

CONTENTS

INTRODUCTION

Steinbeck said in *The Grapes of Wrath* that it is the female of the species who passes heritage and culture and a sense of family down through the generations. Throughout history, using textiles as the medium and their hands as the tools, our ancestors have created beauty and humble art. Today we are awed by the creations of another time and place: the intertwining threads of a piece of old lace, the lines and colors of a bird embroidered in Eastern European cross stitch, and the threads deftly adorning silk and linen. We imagine another time when pride in simple things like home and hearth existed alongside the difficulties of the day. We imagine women who must have been like us.

In this new century, we, too, care about art and color, form and style, hearth and home, and a job well done. We want to do more than just admire the vintage handwork brought out for special occasions. We want to incorporate it into our lifestyle and enjoy the luxury of old fibers and beauty that were created years ago. Our hands can be used to build upon the creations of women who have gone before us. We can transform and re-create old textiles to bring beauty to our lives, and at the same time contribute to our heritage, culture, and family. We can imagine pride in simple things like home and hearth existing alongside the difficulties of our day.

My passion for sewing is rooted in my personal heritage, my childhood. A familiar sight was my mother at the sewing machine, creating functional, practical items for her children and home, and as time and energy permitted, the humble art that fueled her passion. This passion I share with my mother grew through touch and exploration with my hands. Take fabric, for example. I find I slip it between my fingers, pass it from hand to hand, rub it against my face, and even smell it. I bunch it up and shake it out, flip it over. I use words in my vocabulary like smooth and scratchy, I talk of the fabric's "hand." When the fabric doesn't feel quite right, I hear myself say it needs more texture, more dimension. Almost always, these are unconscious actions, unconscious words. I am a tactile learner.

When I was interviewing for admission to physical therapy school, I was asked why I wanted to become a physical therapist. My answer seemed perfectly logical: I wanted a profession that allowed me to use my hands in a creative way to help people. Perhaps the confidence with which I expressed this desire was rooted in a passion for creating with my hands, which had been passed down through my ancestors and had been evolving inside of me for years.

Working with vintage linens has been a connection to the past for me. Writing this book as been a lofty goal, one rooted in the desire to connect with the future, to share my joy for this craft of creating beauty from vintage textiles with other like-minded enthusiasts.

The techniques and projects I explain in this book and the creative ideas I throw out are aimed at getting you going in the direction of trying something new with something old. By accepting the imperfect nature of the vintage textile, and by extension, ourselves, I hope some of the fear of creating with our hands will disappear. We can all create beauty and art through the work of our hands to document our lives and to share with our families. Along the way we're bound to discover a little about the way we learn, the choices we make, and the passions we enjoy.

CHAPTER ONE

DISCOVERING VINTAGE TREASURES

Vintage textiles can be fragile, damaged, and limited in quantity, and like antique furniture, acquire a patina with age. The faded or yellowed color of a vintage fabric or lace compares to the faded and chipping paint from an old bench, the texture softened from years of wear. And like antique furniture, vintage textiles can be a welcome addition to our lives, bringing a sense of luxury and history into a contemporary lifestyle.

Combining vintage textiles into garment construction and home decor may require more flexibility and perhaps a different approach than when working with new fabrics, but the end result is a one-of-a-kind creation. Let's begin by determining what to look for in vintage linens, and how and where to find them. We'll discuss the cleaning and pressing requirements of the vintage textiles in preparation for the creative work.

FINDING VINTAGE TEXTILES

So where do you find vintage textiles, how do you know what you've found, and how do you care for it once you have it? Once you start looking, you'll realize how much is out there, waiting for you to find it. Every yard sale, flea market, and antiques shop is a possible source; even your own attic may be able to provide you with wonderful fabric for future projects. Here are some guidelines to finding and choosing fabrics, and how to be sure that what you have selected will hold up under the stresses of being transformed into a wonderful creation for you or your home.

This was my first attempt at sewing with vintage linens (not counting doll clothes). I made this blouse in the '70s from a dresser scarf and ribbon.

Educate Yourself

Whether you are an experienced collector or you prefer to fly by the seat of your pants, begin by exploring books devoted to vintage textiles. In addition to becoming a more savvy consumer, you will develop a greater appreciation and love for the art and craft of our ancestors. Educate yourself about what you like. Visit antiques stores and museums that feature such exhibits; I viewed the one at Ellis Island, in New York, and was amazed and inspired by the beautiful and varied textiles brought by immigrants at the turn of the century. Exposure to fine textiles and the variety of their designs will teach your eye to appreciate beautiful design and workmanship.

Study prices to get a sense of market value of antique pieces, and talk to dealers, who generally like to share their knowledge and may be able to help you find what you want. Peruse clothing catalogs and magazines for styles that inspire you. Interior-design

Beautiful needle-point pieces, often unfinished, can be found at estate sales and flea markets. This one became wearable art.

magazines and books often show vintage textiles, and home decorating, crafts, and sewing television programs showcase projects using vintage pieces. Finally, old magazines and books will give you insight into how the creators of these textiles used them.

Where to Look

While the popularity of all things old continues to increase, you can still find vintage textiles at reasonable prices. If you haven't inherited textiles, or you don't want to cut up family heirlooms, don't despair. Check the yellow pages and the Internet for places selling vintage items. (See Resources on p. 133.) Frequent antiques stores, fairs, flea markets, and consignment and thrift stores. If you don't see what you are looking for, ask; dealers and shop owners don't always display all their goods. Visiting these sites can be part of your vacation plans, and checking your local newspaper for estate sales, garage sales, and church bazaars can be fun. Ask your friends—often they have family pieces they would gladly give to someone who appreciates them.

Even those vintage treasures that appear to defy recycling can provide creative inspiration.

My sister told me I had gone over the edge when I bought the tablecloth used for this shirt. "It is so faded!" Exactly why I loved it!

How to Look

Once you have found sources, arm yourself with the proper equipment: tape measure, magnifying glass, flashlight, pattern yardage guidelines, and color requirements. Keep a list of the vintage and new textiles you already own and bring swatches and samples, because in the throes of creative overload, it is easy to forget what you have or need.

What to Look For

Use vintage textiles in your creations, but bypass expensive antiques. If the textile is an antique that has historical value or significance to you, don't put it on the cutting table. The vintage treasures to look for are old linens such as tablecloths, doilies, and embroidered towels, as well as old fabrics, quilts, and curtains. With your imagination, recycled cloth-

The word "vintage" is used to describe something that is old, a classic. An heirloom is an inherited family piece.

The pattern for this blouse emphasizes the beauty of the Irish linen tablecloth. The pin was made by my sister who used an old Bakelite button.

The possibilities of vintage fabrics you can transform into wearables are endless— from draperies to knitted sweaters to handkerchiefs.

ing such as ties, furs, kimonos, and sweaters, old bits of laces and trims, handkerchiefs, buttons, and beads can be incorporated into your creations. They may be 100 years old or 10 years old.

In your search at vintage shops or thrift stores, look for anything that catches your fancy and not likely to be found in a fabric store. Color, texture, handwork, or the unusual nature of the piece may attract you. I have blouses made from lime-green tablecloths, and from old Irish linens as soft as butter, with collars from embroidery rarely equaled. Bear in mind what you would like to create, but remain open to creative inspiration.

If you find something you really like buy it, even if you don't know how to use it. Take it home and tack it to a prominent wall, or put it with other favorite fabrics you own; inspira-

tion is likely to strike. Sometimes something as awful as a bright pumpkin-colored dress made of cheap polyester from the '50s but embellished with lovely beadwork will tempt you to creative heights. If you love the bead-work, it will find its way to your worktable.

Vintage Treasures to Consider

Choose vintage textiles with fabrics, colors, designs, and treasures you love. Look for:

+ Braids and trims
+ Buttons and beads
+ Draperies
+ Dresser and piano scarves
+ Dresses, sweaters, coats, and old furs
+ Ethnic textiles
+ Fabric yard goods
+ Hand and kitchen towels
+ Handkerchiefs

- Kimonos, obis, and kimono fabric pieces
- Knitted and crocheted pieces such as afghans, hats, and gloves
- Laces
- Purses
- Quilts, pieced quilt tops, and quilt blocks
- Silk ties
- Tablecloths and napkins
- Wool needlepoint pieces

CHOOSING A VINTAGE TREASURE

Once you discover where to find textiles, remember that not everything will suit your purpose. Your plans for the vintage textile will determine, in part, its suitability. A vintage textile to be used for a garment will need to be in good condition, with quality workmanship and materials. On the other hand, a slightly damaged textile, one of lesser quality, or one that is fragile may be fine as a decorative item.

Quality of Workmanship and Materials

When you find a vintage piece that catches your eye, examine it carefully. Assess the quality of the fabric, threads, trims, and buttons. No matter how beautiful the embroidery work, when done on poor-quality cotton it will always be a disappointment, and it may not hold up to the rigors of reworking. Look at the quality of the workmanship as well as the quality of the materials.

Examine the front and back of the piece. Hand stitching tends to be less perfectly executed than machine stitching. The back of a hand-embroidered piece will have threads passing randomly from design to design while the back of machine work is highly regular. Small, evenly spaced and neat-looking hand stitches were probably stitched by a talented needleworker. The quality of the vintage piece is further enhanced when color, fabric, and

design have been combined in an appealing manner. Unusual details added to the vintage piece, such as hand-stitched buttonholes and piping, add interest and character.

In the end, the importance of quality workmanship and materials is a function of how the vintage piece will be used. When I decided to make simple slipcovers for my dining-room chairs, I wanted embroidered vintage linens as the focus, therefore the workmanship of the embroidery as well as the fabric needed to be high quality (see the photo below). Using damaged or lesser-quality vintage textiles for this project wouldn't have made sense, but the workmanship in a small or damaged piece can still be admired if made into a small pillow or a gift bag for a bottle of wine (see the project on pp. 34–35).

Finding the Right Piece

In your search for the perfect vintage textile, keep your intended project in mind and ask yourself the questions on p. 10.

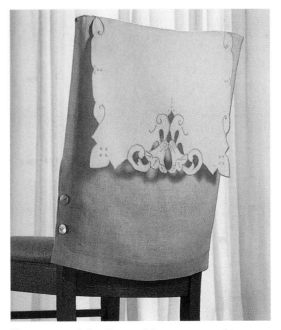

The center of the linen table runner used to make this slipcover was stained with what looked like wine, but the corners with beautiful embroidery were undamaged.

Taking advantage of its lovely design, I cut a red and black vintage silk scarf into pieces and inserted them into this kimono-style jacket. The large vintage button covers a snap on the jacket's underside.

✦ Are you looking for an embellishment or something for an entire project? Does the vintage piece coordinate with or complement fabric you already own? How much fabric will you be able to salvage from the vintage piece?

✦ Is the design appealing? The vintage textile may have an overall design, as in a damask tablecloth, or areas of limited design, as in the embroidered corners of a napkin. Consider the use: A damask tablecloth can add impact to the beauty of a blouse when the design is strategically placed, while the embroidered corner of a napkin is useful in a detail such as a pocket or collar.

✦ Do you like the color and/or the color combinations? From the pale color of old lace to the rich colors found in a vintage silk scarf, it is often the color that makes the piece right.

✦ The weight, texture, stability, and drape of the fabric also should work well with the style you have in mind. Heavyweight linen may be just the right choice for a jacket but not a blouse.

The wine bag is stained and the embroidery on the sachets less than perfect, but who cares? They still make a beautiful presentation.

✦ Is the size of the vintage piece too large or too small? Is the size of the pattern on the fabric the correct scale for your project? If you are considering lace, trim, or buttons, are their scale correct for your project?

✦ Does the hand of the fabric appeal to you? If you find yourself stroking a piece of fabric, buy it!

✦ Appreciate the "sense" of the vintage piece. If you want a '40s-style blouse, do the color, pattern, and texture of the vintage piece evoke this feeling?

✦ Will the vintage piece you are considering hold up to the rigors of your lifestyle (the kids, the dog, and the laundry)? For garment construction, choose pieces that will tolerate frequent laundering and require manageable ironing. Purchase and use more delicate pieces for sachets, pillows, purses, wall hangings, dolls, and other infrequently laundered projects.

A simple blouse pattern highlights the beauty of the pale pink damask tablecloth. I omitted the darts to avoid disturbing the damask design.

The lace used on this blouse was originally attached to two pieces of fine cotton batiste that probably served as a curtain for a small window.

Overall Condition of Vintage Treasures

Before purchasing your piece, make a close inspection; items at these shops usually aren't returnable. How does the textile look, feel, and smell? Hold it up to the light, or shine your flashlight through it and check for worn areas, holes, rust spots, stains, and moth or insect damage. Are the stains and holes repairable?

As you hold a piece up to the light, look around the edges and inspect the embroidery. Has the color from the embroidery threads bled into the fabric? This is hard to fix, but if the piece is really beautiful, you may decide to buy it anyway and find a way to use it, perhaps combining it with other vintage pieces and overdyeing (dyeing a second time) the whole thing or piecing it into a garment.

Consider silk vintage textiles carefully, as the delicate nature of this fabric presents challenges when stained or ripped and is especially vulnerable to perspiration damage. For other textiles, check to see if the color has faded. If so, do you like the look, or would the fabric take dye well?

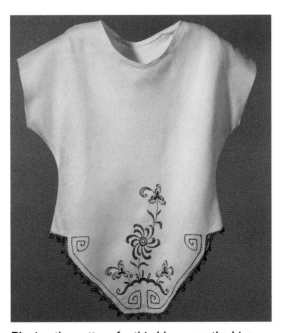

Placing the pattern for this blouse on the bias resulted in a softer drape and allowed the pattern to fit onto a small square tablecloth. The hem was shaped to follow the lines of the tablecloth, leaving the handwork undisturbed.

Inspect crochet work, needlepoint, knitting, and tatting for pulled or broken threads and work integrity. Don't be afraid to ask family and friends who have needlework skills for help in the repair process.

If you notice a musty smell, it may be a sign of mildew damage, and washing the piece can result in large rips and holes. But if there are no visible mildew spots and it's especially wonderful, take a chance.

Considering Cost

Like anything else, the price of vintage textiles is determined by the perceived value in the marketplace. While the quality of the workmanship, the materials used, and the overall condition of the piece are important in determining price, so are the laws of supply and demand and where they are purchased. When

One of my favorite blouse collars was made from a tablecloth that was stained and had holes throughout except for two corners containing the most exquisite embroidery. (Spring Street pattern from The Sewing Workshop.)

floral tablecloths from the '50s are featured in home-decorating magazines and on television, their popularity drives the supply down and the cost up. The tablecloth purchased at an antiques store in New York City will be more expensive than a similar one in Topeka, Kansas. The best bargain will be found at a local church bazaar or garage sale because you won't be forced to pay the cost of the middle man.

In the end, value is in the eye of the beholder. Is the cost something you can live with? Unfortunately for us sewers, cost can be a stumbling block. After all, if we spend a lot of money in addition to effort and time on a creation that turns out to be a disappointment, we may be reluctant to try again. Find a vintage treasure that appeals to you *and* is reasonably priced, then let the creative juices flow. A failed creative venture is not nearly as painful when you have little money invested, and successfully incorporating an inexpensive vintage piece into your design makes you feel especially clever.

Once You Decide to Buy

When you've found the item you want, look it over carefully. Remember you are purchasing a finite commodity. Be a wise buyer and:

- ✦ Look for multiples, whether identical or matching, and buy as many of them as you can afford. If there is pair, buy them both. If you are buying buttons, buy them all.
- ✦ Bargain if you think the piece is overpriced, but keep in mind the vendor is just trying to make a living. If you are taking a chance with a damaged vintage textile, point this out in your negotiations.
- ✦ Do it. You've seen the signs: "The time to buy an antique is now"; you may not get another chance.

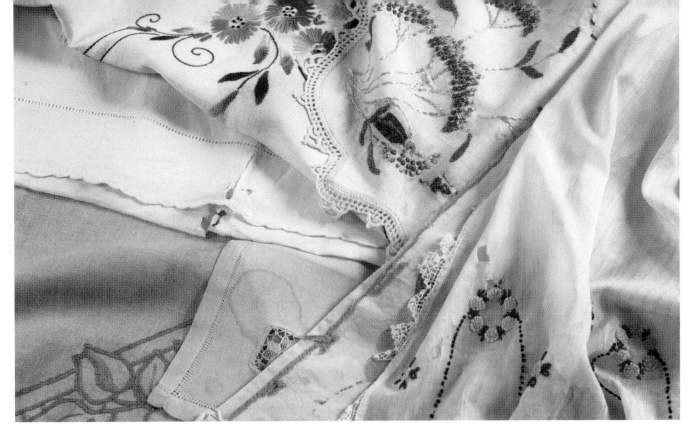

CLEANING VINTAGE TEXTILES

Don't bring a vintage purchase into your home until you're ready to inspect and launder it. You don't know where it has been stored, how it has been cared for, or what insects or creatures have previously or presently inhabit it.

If you are unable to deal with your purchase immediately, put it into a plastic, zipper-type bag, then into a plastic container with a tight-fitting lid, and into the freezer. This process will kill, or at least contain, any bugs that might have contaminated your vintage purchase. Just remember to remove it before your mother visits—imagine my mother's horror a few years ago when a container of fur collars fell out of the freezer and promptly spilled its contents at her feet!

Looking for Flaws and Stains

To prepare the vintage piece for laundering, examine it closely in strong light. Improvise a light table by using a lamp under a glass-topped table and draping the piece over it.

Remove pins or stickers and look closely for flaws and stains. Check the fabric for holes and damaged threads, a sign of moths or insects, and repair them if possible. To the extent possible, repair torn lace, crochet, and embroidery damage. Secure any loose threads, which may unravel in the wash, with a zigzag stitch or a serged edge. Locate and mark stains with straight pins or sticky notes.

Stain Removal

There are many sources available for guidance in treating stains. Scores of household hints-and-tips books are currently on the market; cleaning products from the supermarket usually provide contact information for additional advice. Books on antique and vintage textiles are a good source; even cookbooks, particularly the style produced by various women's groups, offer stain-removal suggestions. Ask your mother or grandmother how she would handle a problem; sometimes the old methods really are best. About 25 years ago I acquired a diary of sorts, dated 1947, author unknown, containing information important to the author such as the cost of running the farm (cost of chicks, chicken feed, cost of doctor visits) and recipes for pickles, filling floor cracks, preventing laundry from freezing on the clothesline, and for whitening laundry (see the photo below).

Part of the beauty and allure of the vintage textile is that it has had a previous life, and as such, will not be perfect. Stains may be a permanent part of the vintage textile, and you may need to work around them. Having said this, you will probably still want to begin your project with your fabric, lace, or linen in as pristine condition as possible.

Suggested techniques for stain removal follow and should be attempted with caution. I don't work with priceless, antique textiles and it's a good thing: I have had my share of stain removal attempts that resulted in further destruction of the cloth. Far more frequently, however, I've used sometimes fairly aggressive cleaning techniques and added a little creativity to recycle old finds into new treasures.

Identifying stains Identifying a stain will help determine the type of cleaner to use, but this may not be possible in all cases, so make an educated guess:

+ Water-based stains can be caused by coffee, vinegar, or other beverages and leave brown spots.
+ Soft drinks, fruit juices, and alcoholic beverages frequently cause acid-based stains. Acid stains cause the fabrics to discolor and the fibers to deteriorate, especially on cotton, rayon, and ramie fibers.
+ Many offenders, including cooking oils, butter, salad dressings, cosmetics, and car grease cause oil-based stains. Oil stains tend to follow the weave of the fabric and often produce yellow discoloration.
+ Perspiration stains can cause dyes to bleed, while antiperspirants left on fabric can result in crystallized stains, fading or yellowing, and weakened fibers.
+ Protein offenders such as blood, baby formula, and chocolate tend to leave brown stains.
+ Iron or rust damage from pins or metal hangers can result in brown or yellow stains.

Treating stains Sometimes all that is needed to remove water-and acid-based stains from a washable fabric is a simple soak or wash. Dissolve a mild soap in tepid water in a large basin and, unless the vintage textiles are all similar in color, soak only one at a time for 20 to 30 minutes. At the end of the soak, let the water drain and add more water, rinsing and draining until the water runs clear. If you are not afraid of shrinkage or fibers felting a little, you can treat wool this way. Keep the water temperature constant and cool and do not agitate the wool, as this can result in fiber distortion and felting.

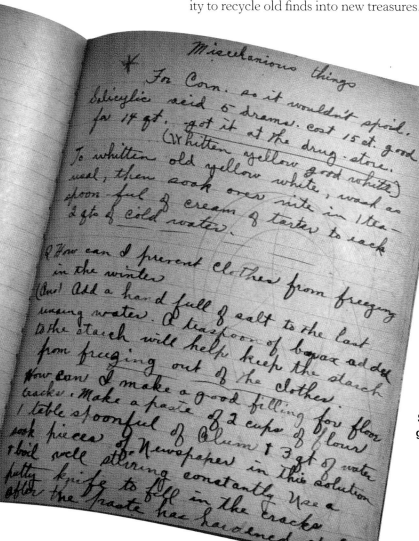

Sometimes the oldest advice is the best: I found great tips from this 50-year-old household diary.

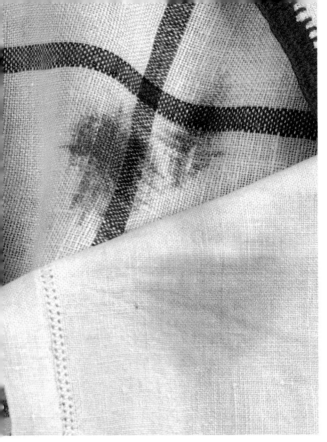

Consider the stain: The protein stain on the top sample may not come out, but chances are the oil stain on the one below will.

Try removing oil-based stains by moistening the spot with a dilution of 1 part ammonia to 3 parts water, then sandwich the stain between two pieces of blotting paper or absorbent cloths and iron it dry (see the photo at right). Repeat as necessary. If this does not work, the stain can be treated with a commercial dry-cleaning solvent. It can be purchased at dry cleaners, shoe-repair shops, and some grocery stores. Lightly spray the stained area, then gently blot with a clean, white cloth. Repeat as needed.

Perspiration stains can sometimes be removed or diminished by applying a prewash stain remover. If perspiration has changed the color of the fabric, applying a white-vinegar solution (1 part vinegar to 3 parts water) directly to an old stain may help. Rinse and wash in the hottest water possible.

Protein stains, such as chocolate and blood stains, can be removed with enzyme-based presoak products. Enzymes aid in breaking down complex soils, especially proteins.

A mild bleach solution for soaking may also be effective. When using bleach, follow the manufacturer's directions, but be aware that these products may damage a delicate piece.

Chlorine bleach can be used on washable natural fibers including linen and cotton, but is not compatible with wool, silk, and some dyes. To determine if a fabric is chlorine-bleach safe, make a solution of 1 tablespoon of chlorine bleach to ¼ cup water and apply one drop of the test solution in an inconspicuous area, such as a seam allowance or hem. Allow the solution to penetrate the fabric for one minute, then blot dry with a paper towel. If the color does not bleed or change color, bleach is theoretically safe to use.

Non-chlorine bleach or oxygen bleach produces a gentler bleaching action than chlorine bleach and can be safely used on many fabrics and colors, but again, try in an inconspicuous area. Make a solution of 1 teaspoon dry oxygen bleach to 1 cup hot water. Place a few drops of solution in an inconspicuous area and look for color change or bleeding. Be aware that any of these products may damage a delicate piece, however, so use caution.

Treat brown or yellow discoloration from iron or rust with a commercial rust-removal

Make sure the cloth you use to blot the stain is white. A colored blotting cloth can impart dyes into the vintage fabric.

product, following the manufacturer's instructions. Do not use bleach—doing so may intensify the stain.

Mildew has a distinctive smell of mold, and can leave a green-gray cast to the fabric and cause fiber destruction. If mildew damage is not too extensive, it may be possible to remove it through fairly aggressive methods, being sure to try the technique in an inconspicuous area first. If the fabric can tolerate it, launder the stained items using chlorine bleach, adding ½ cup bleach per load to the washing machine.

Overall whitening and deodorizing A mild chlorine-bleach-and-water solution can produce overall whitening and deodorizing for some vintage fabrics. Begin by using a weaker version of the bleach manufacturer's recipe and test it in an inconspicuous location on the fabric. Whether I use chlorine bleach, or the more gentle nonchlorine or oxygen bleach, for overall whitening and deodorizing, I decrease the manufacturer's suggested amount of bleach by 25 percent to minimize the likelihood of damage to the vintage textiles.

Choosing the Best Cleaning Method

With the stains pretreated to your satisfaction, it is time to move on to washing the whole textile. What are your choices? There are many opinions about which methods work best, so choose what works for you. Treat the piece as you plan to treat it after construction. The most common methods for cleaning vintage linens that tolerate wet cleaning include machine washing on gentle cycle, and hand washing. For fabrics that do not tolerate wet cleaning, try professional assistance from a reputable dry cleaner. Additionally, home dry-cleaning products are available for dry-clean-only fabrics. Consider the factors affecting the choice of cleaning method: fabric content, fabric strength, colorfastness, and the desired outcome.

If you decide you need a professional dry cleaner, be certain you know and trust their work. Consider taking the vintage textile to a professional who has expertise in working with specialty textiles.

Home dry-cleaning products are designed to give consumers similar results of professional dry cleaning containing similar products, while at the same time allowing you more control over the outcome. To use this product, apply the stain remover to the vintage piece, then place it in the provided bag and place it in the dryer for 30 minutes. These products should be used cautiously, however, as they are recommended for "dry clean only" fabrics and require medium to high dryer heat, which could further damage the vintage textile.

Fabric content Cotton, linen, polyester, and blends generally tolerate laundering with detergents, cold to warm water, and stain-

These curtains looked fine before they were washed, but afterward it was clear they had suffered damage from the sun.

removal products. Silk can shrink and stain when exposed to water, and detergents and stain-removing products may remove the fabric dye. Wool can be washed safely in cool water without agitation and temperature changes, but shrinking is always a concern.

Fabric strength Test the strength of a fabric when considering the best method for cleaning. Tightly woven fabrics with a heftier hand, such as linen and heavier cottons, have greater strength or integrity than very thin silks or fine cotton batiste. Fabrics damaged from repeated washings, mildew, sunlight, or age will have poor strength. Applying strong stain removers to already weakened fabric can cause it to rip (see the photo on the facing page).

Colorfastness With vintage textiles that have been washed repeatedly, chances of the color running are slim, but you never know. Wash like colors together or when in doubt, wash each textile separately. For linens with brightly colored embroidery thread, pretest colorfastness by pressing a moist towel into the threads in an inconspicuous area and watching for evidence of the color bleeding. Commercial products that prevent colors from running or bleeding can be added to the wash water.

Choosing an outcome How do you want your vintage textile to look after you've cleaned it? Do you want it to look the same but cleaner? Minimize shrinking, stretching, and distortion when washing by keeping the water temperature cool and by placing the vintage piece in a mesh laundry bag, or, if it is large, inside a white pillowcase basted shut. Dissolve a mild detergent in the water before adding the vintage textile and wash on the gentle cycle, or hand-wash if the item is delicate or does not need frequent washing. A very fragile textile can be hand-washed by merely soaking it in cool water with the appropriate detergents

TEA DYEING

Sometimes the beauty of a vintage textile is in the yellow or ecru color it has assumed. If you are overly diligent and the vintage piece becomes too white and pristine with washing, try using a dye from the supermarket or a tea dye to regain that ecru tint.

To make tea dye, boil enough water to accommodate the size of the piece. Add tea bags (start with 8 to 10 per gallon of water), steep until the desired color is achieved, then remove the tea bags. When the water has cooled to the touch, soak the textile in the tea bath until the fabric is slightly darker than what you want and rinse the fabric in cold water. It will become a lighter color when dry.

Be aware that stains will not be removed by dyeing and in fact may be enhanced with the addition of color.

Vintage textiles embellished with beading, ribbon work, and embroidery may be made up of different fabrics, so test the cleaning method in an inconspicuous area first.

Cleaning a fragile textile can mean simply soaking it in a mild detergent.

until it has had time to produce the desired effect (see the photo on p. 17). Rinse in cool water without agitating, blot excess water with towels, and air-dry.

Drying

Heat can be an unnecessary evil to vintage textiles, causing fiber damage and distortion. Air-drying is less stressful, as long as the weight of the wet textile is supported. Hanging wet textiles over a line or on a hanger can result in stretched and distorted fibers. Use two upright drying racks pushed together to support the weight of the drying textile. Air-dry large pieces like quilts, tablecloths, and bedspreads by placing them on a sheet on the floor, out of direct sunlight.

PRESSING

Whether you are sewing with new or vintage fabrics and textiles, pressing is vital to the final outcome. Press throughout construction to achieve professional-looking results. Use caution when pressing vintage textiles, and take into consideration the fragile nature and unusual characteristics of each piece.

The Right Pressing Equipment

Iron vintage textiles on a well-padded ironing board that is free from stains. When working with a large piece such as a tablecloth or a sheet, support the weight of the draping fabric on a chair placed next to the ironing board. Before you iron, clean the iron according to the manufacturer's directions to release any mineral buildup, and clean the soleplate with a cleaner to remove any buildup of starch, detergent, fabric fibers, or other residue (see the top photo on the facing page).

You may not know the fabric content of the vintage piece, so test press in an inconspicuous area. Make a conservative estimate of the iron temperature, starting with a medium-cool setting, and increasing as needed. Pre-

✦ *To prevent fringe on a vintage piece from tangling during laundering, roll the piece so the fringe is tucked in on the inside. Then secure the roll with a rubber band. If the fringe still gets tangled, try combing it gently.*

✦ *To hand-wash a quilt or other large piece, fill a bathtub with tepid water and add a small amount of gentle liquid laundry soap. To support the weight of the quilt, lay it on a white sheet and lower it into the water. Let it soak for 30 minutes, then gently squeeze the water through the quilt. When the water is dirty or cloudy, change it, repeating until the water becomes clear; a handheld shower nozzle helps get the soap out. Drain the tub and squeeze out as much excess water as possible before removing the quilt. Roll the quilt in white towels to further squeeze out water. Dry the quilt on a clean sheet or mattress pad, out of the direct sunlight.*

✦ *If you can't press clean linens right away, dampen them slightly, place them in a plastic, zipper-type bag, and refrigerate. When you are ready to iron, they will still be damp.*

✦ *Wash like colors and fabrics together. Wash fibers that shed separately.*

heat the iron for at least 15 minutes as some irons heat up to the maximum temperature first before cooling down to the desired temperature.

Use steam and water cautiously when ironing. Too much steam can damage fibers, causing them to shrink and tear, and water can leave spots, especially on silk. Use a press cloth between the iron and the vintage piece to protect from heat and water damage. A variety of press cloths, including semitransparent ones, are available commercially. You can also use doctor's exam paper, which provides a semitransparent, protective barrier and is available in rolls from a medical-supply store.

To further prevent scorches, a soleplate cover can be attached, although it can hinder steam penetration and catch residue between the cover and the soleplate (see Resources on p. 133).

Special Handling

To maintain the raised surfaces of lace and embroidery, place the piece wrong side up over a Turkish towel or velvet board. Cover with a press cloth and gently press, using an up-and-down motion (see the bottom photo at right). Use a damp press cloth if you have checked for colorfastness and you aren't pressing silk. Keep checking to see when the piece is pressed to your satisfaction.

If the fabric is especially soft, delicate, or flimsy, spraying it with starch when ironing adds stability to the cloth, making it easier to cut out and sew up. However, if you are not going to work the cloth into a new design soon, leave the starch out. Starched fabrics tend to attract insects and have a tendency to absorb moisture, which may cause mildew. Additionally, heavily starched laces and linens can become brittle and tear.

Combining vintage textiles with new fabrics presents extra challenges for the home sewer. Mixing the old with the new may result

Before working with vintage linens, clean your iron thoroughly, then frequently throughout the sewing project.

Press embroidered and lacy fabrics wrong side up, over a Turkish towel or velvet board, gently moving the iron up and down and checking the fabric frequently.

in different heat and water requirements, and require some trial and error to determine the best way to press. Set the iron temperature for the most heat-sensitive fiber. Use a press cloth judiciously, and heat and water cautiously.

I am the first to admit that I have not always followed these guidelines. Through inept ironing, I have seen splotchy drops and scorch marks appear on more than one occasion. Once, during a final pressing of a nearly completed white blouse, I created a spot on the front. I quickly soaked the blouse in mild detergent and returned it to the washing machine. The blouse was fine. Remember that while the fabrics being used are vintage pieces, they are not priceless antiques. You have given them new life, and they need to survive the rigors of your lifestyle.

POTPOURRI BAGS

A few years ago I discovered the most wonderful orange-vanilla potpourri mixture. I put it in bowls in almost every room, but because my family tends to be clumsy, the potpourri was always spilling. One afternoon, I gathered some vintage tablecloth and fabric pieces, laces, and buttons and made little bags to hold the potpourri. They look great grouped together and make nice gifts. This is a good way to use the unspoiled parts of damaged or stained linens, or fragile pieces that seem beyond repair. Make bags in any shape or size for this fast, easy project. Incorporate a beautiful edge, lovely embroidery, or vintage buttons and beads into the design.

Potpourri bags made from scraps of vintage fabric bring beauty and fragrance to any room.

MATERIALS

* *Vintage textile cut into 6 in. by 6 in.*
* *Buttons, beads, baubles*
* *Potpourri mixture of your choice*

1. For a 5-in. square bag, cut two pieces of fabric 6 in. by 6 in.

2. Embellish the fabric pieces as desired. Attach lace in the seams or stitch randomly across the square of fabric. Add buttons, beads, or ribbons in a pattern of your design. Create dimension by stacking beads onto buttons, or smaller buttons onto larger buttons and sewing them onto the fabric. Add a vintage pin. Stamp

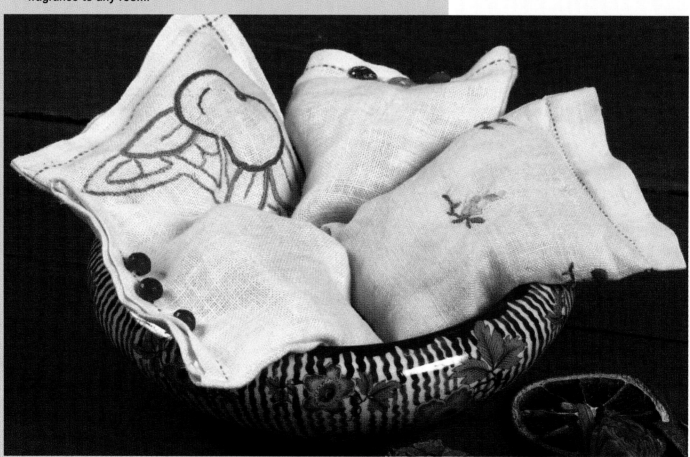

or stencil the squares of fabric, or add small tassels to the corners.

3. Place the right sides of the squares together and pin. Using a ½-in. seam allowance, sew around the square leaving a 3-in. opening at the center of one edge.

4. Turn the bag right side out and press the edges. Fill the bag loosely with potpourri.

5. Hand-stitch or machine topstitch the opening closed. Do not place the bag directly on clothes or wood, because the oils from the potpourri may cause damage. Add more embellishments if desired.

STEP 1 **Cut two pieces of fabric, 6 in. square.**

STEP 2 **Decorate the bag with beads, buttons, or fabric paint.**

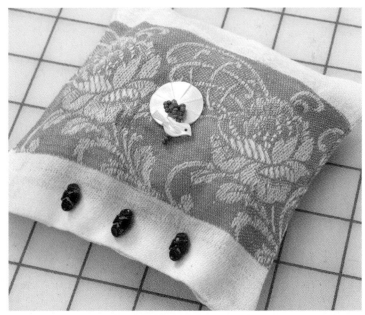

STEP 5 **After filling the bag with potpourri, stitch the opening closed. Add a faux button closure if you like.**

CHAPTER TWO

DESIGN AND CONSTRUCTION

Most sewers are comfortable choosing a commercial pattern and constructing a garment according to the instructions. They find the pattern they like and purchase the recommended amount and type of fabric, adjusting for size and sewing it up the way they're instructed.

While sewing with vintage textiles requires some adjustments to this familiar scenario, the basic sewing skills you now possess will serve you well when you want to spread your wings. The goal is to incorporate the vintage textile into the design of your new garment, or more creatively, to receive the inspiration from the vintage pieces for the design. Once you select or develop a design, you should then review and adapt the construction sequence and recommended sewing techniques and procedures. In this chapter, you'll learn to become confident in choosing design and construction methods that work with vintage textiles.

The wool needlepoint used as an inset in the back of this vest was paired with equally heavy fabric, in this case, wool melton.

Machine-embroidered vintage cotton lace for the jacket collar was paired with handkerchief-weight linen in this Mission Top pattern from The Sewing Workshop.

GETTING INSPIRED

Take design inspiration from your vintage textile. Drape the piece over a dress form or chair, step back, and take in the whole picture. The type of fabric, and the pattern, as well as color, style, and details of the vintage piece may all provide inspiration. Let's look at these.

Fabric

Pairing fabric with design is a crucial element for the home sewer and sometimes a difficult connection to make. The fiber content, weight, texture, and drape of the fabric will have a direct bearing on how the vintage textile will look once it's made up—wool bouclè or coarse linen, both highly textural and heavy, bring to mind a different design than lightweight, gauzy cotton or slippery silk. It's difficult to achieve a soft neckline with stiff linen, and equally hard to structure a slippery silk into sharp, tailored details.

Start by thinking about the specific garment. If you want to make a blouse, pull out your favorite one and look at the fabric and design critically. What is it about the combination of design and fabric that appeals to you? Compare similarities between the vintage textile and the fabric in your favorite blouse. For example, a soft rayon tablecloth might have drape and a similar weight to three-ply silk, and both suggest an unstructured, soft design. Keep in mind the way the fabric drapes, and don't try to force it to do something else.

If you plan to use the vintage textile as an accent to pair with another fabric, consider the compatibility of the pieces. Generally, the weight of the fabrics, their contents, and textures should be similar, and the laundering and pressing requirements compatible. For example, pairing embroidered cotton lace with handkerchief-weight linen is a good

ASSESSING THE FABRIC

Drape the vintage textile over your body in front of a long mirror or over a dress form. Step back, and take in the whole picture.

When you look at the whole effect, does it suggest the need for a second fabric to either emphasize or tone down the vintage textile? Does the drape on the form suggest ideas for garments? A jacket or blouse design may come to mind, but don't stop at the first concept! Imagine less obvious designs like a skirt or the front and back panel of a dress or jumper.

Does the fall of the fabric emphasize angles or curves, or is there a neckline fold that suggests a collar treatment?

What was it that attracted you to the vintage piece? The embroidered ends of a dresser scarf given three-dimensional shape over the dress form may inspire a design.

Do surface embellishment ideas such as beading or button placement become more apparent with the fabric draped?

Put your project to bed over the dress form and when you see it the next morning, your vision will have more clarity.

Once you see the possibilities, sketch the emerging design, or enlarge the line drawings from a pattern you like and play with the design. Consider this process a little like doodling. Your drawings don't have to be accurate or close to your final design but they may be helpful in giving you a creative start and concrete form to your ideas.

Continue to drape your project throughout the process to help clarify and modify your design.

I like the way the scalloped edge lies along the neckline of the dress form. I will try to incorporate that information into the design of the garment.

choice. Both fabrics are lightweight, smooth textured, and somewhat stiff, and both are washable and require similar heat settings on the iron (see the bottom photo on p. 24). If you pair a vintage textile with a fabric that just doesn't seem right, trust your instincts and try another combination.

But you don't always have to follow these guidelines. If what you like seems to break all the rules, try it anyway; it may be one of the reasons you sew. You may not be able to find a fabric similar to your vintage textile, or you may really fall in love with the combination of wool suiting and silk charmeuse cowboy fabric. It may be the surprise element of the combination that you're after, or it just may be that you know what you like.

With any combination, however, you should interface, launder, and press the completed garment, taking into consideration

The damask tablecloth gave a subtle tone-on-tone design to this pink blouse. An added bonus: The texture is great against the skin.

The tablecloth used to make this '50s style camp shirt is a lush green that reminds me of the kitchen colors of my youth.

the individual fabrics. Make a sample of your fabric combination. If you have a silk and wool combination, for instance, consider using a sew-in interfacing like silk organza for the silk fabric and a fusible interfacing for the wool fabric. The silk organza interfacing will provide soft support to the silk without requiring heat, and fusible interfacing will be an easy and effective way to give needed body to the wool. Select the lower silk heat setting when pressing the garment to avoid damaging the more delicate silk and use a press cloth to avoid a wool shine.

Several hankies were cut in half, pieced together, and sewn into box pleats along the bottom edge of this blouse.

Color

Take inspiration from the colors of the vintage textiles. Colors may be bright and lively or subdued and faded. Whichever your preference, it is probable that color is what first caught your eye. Consider how the colors make you feel, and use this information when designing your garment.

The vintage textile you love may be multicolored, as in ties and handkerchiefs. Others have a tone-on-tone design, as seen in a damask tablecloth or a natural linen dresser scarf embroidered with ecru floss. Tone-on-tone colors lend themselves well to an entire garment and suggest a simple, sophisticated design (see the top photo on the facing page). Making an entire blouse out of a collection of multicolored hankies, on the other hand, would be overwhelming. Instead, I'd use the hankie collection as a design detail, adding the handkerchiefs along the bottom of a white cotton or linen blouse. See the photo above.

Use texture as a unifying element between an accent piece and the rest of the garment. In the example at right, wool melton was a good choice because its heavy, dense texture balanced the highly textural upholstery fabric.

Motif of the Fabric Design

The motif of the fabric design refers to the subject matter. Cherubs floating in flowers, a deck of cards, horses, kittens, or a geometric shape could inspire the design of your garment. The motifs of vintage pieces are often a reflection of our times and culture, and we may react to them strongly. I might fall in love with a vintage piece covered with dancing green peppers and carrots and be inspired to use them as appliqués for a playful jacket. Someone else may find the design unappealing, at best (see the top photo on p. 28).

Scale of the Fabric Design

Scale in a vintage textile refers to the size of the design on the fabric. Flowers can be big or small; stripes wide or narrow; and embroidery patterns confined to one corner or covering an

If you are using a vintage textile as an accent, color may provide direction for the rest of the garment. The pairing of this red vintage upholstery sample with red wool melton creates a vibrant combination.

entire tablecloth. These designs may be woven, embroidered, or sewn into the cloth, or they may be printed on top of the fabric. Generally, making an entire garment out of large-scale patterned fabric isn't flattering, but sometimes the fabric inspires you to do just that.

Style of the Vintage Piece

The style of the vintage piece may bring to mind the period or era when it was produced, and provide inspiration for the design. Victorian textiles embellished with beading, lace, and buttons seem to ooze luxury, while a fur collar from the '50s or '60s reminds us of a Jackie Kennedy-style jacket design. Sometimes the period feel of the vintage piece is so strong that we're inspired to combine it with the unexpected, perhaps a jeans jacket, or a contemporary styled short jacket (see the top photo on the facing page).

Details

Design inspiration can come from the details of vintage textiles and trims such as embroidery, lace, ribbon, beading, heirloom stitching, and even something as simple as the corner of a tablecloth. The variety and availability of vintage buttons make them a great source for design inspiration. If you are having trouble with a design, find an old button and work your design around it. Perhaps the button has a repeating pattern, color, or shape that can be incorporated into the design of a garment (see the photo at right on p. 31).

Or let the embroidery, lace, trim, and

I may be crazy, but I can see those dancing green peppers pieced into the back of a short jacket, embellished with checkered binding and bright vintage buttons.

heirloom stitching inspire a simple blouse with a dramatic collar. Perhaps the placement of embroidery on the corners of a tablecloth will inspire you to use the piece as a focus for the front of a blouse (see the photo at left).

PATTERN SELECTION

Once you have a vintage textile and garment type in mind, pattern selection is simplified. Choose a pattern that suits your style and body type, and keep it simple. Let the beauty of the vintage piece you have selected speak for itself.

Personal Style

In selecting a pattern, first think about your personal style and what looks good on you. Try on different styles of your chosen garment, and take a close look at the design and details. What is it about them you like, and why do they look good on you? Look through magazines and pattern catalogs for ideas.

A blouse design with a front overlay and a back flange highlights the corner embroidery of a tablecloth.

Check out the Internet sites of independent pattern companies for some unusual choices. Can you imagine how your vintage textile would look in any of these designs?

Simple style

Select a simple pattern style to accent the vintage textile. The fashion drawing on the front of the pattern envelope may not be a true representation, so turn the pattern envelope over to see the simplified line drawings. Study the drawings and read the instructions, which show larger line drawings and make details easier to see. Here are some things to look for:

✦ Check the number and complexity of the pattern pieces. Simply styled designs such as boxy blouse, vest, or jacket patterns tend to have fewer pattern pieces and straighter lines.

✦ Patterns without darts, pleats, princess-style seams, tucks, and gathers are a good choice if you want to leave the surface design of the vintage textile intact. For example, if you want to cut a jacket front out of an elaborately embroidered vintage piece, choose a pattern without interrupting seams. On the other hand, if the embroidered piece is to be used for the collar only, details in the jacket body are fine.

✦ Take note of the pattern layout. Chances are you will need to modify or abandon altogether the recommended layout because of the limited amount of fabric you have. In Chapter 3 we'll discuss creative ways to adjust the pattern and layout, so don't get too concerned about fabric shortages yet.

✦ Examine the grainline positions of the pattern pieces. Pattern pieces placed on the bias will have a tendency to stretch or distort, especially if the vintage fabric is loosely woven or fragile, while those placed on

A contemporary-styled jacket pattern was paired with a '50s-style fur collar for an unexpected design.

Take advantage of small-scale geometric patterns, often seen in vintage silk ties, and use them for piping and bias-edge treatments to provide subtle detail, as seen in this jacket.

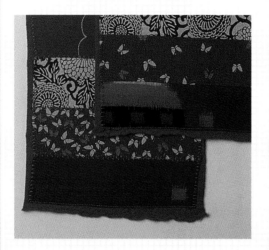

INTERESTING FABRICS MAKE INTERESTING DESIGNS

The variety in colors of vintage kimono textiles creates limitless design possibilities. You can find mail-order vendors who sell vintage kimono fabric on the Internet (see Resources on p. 133). Recycled kimonos from Japan that have been damaged or stained are purchased by companies that take the kimonos apart, remove the damaged areas, and sell coordinated fabric packets by color grouping and size. You select the colors and sizes you want for your garment design. The arrival of a package of exotic fabrics will no doubt send you right to your sewing machine. See chapter 4 for more on appliqué techniques.

Once you've decided on a pattern, make it up first in a fabric that simulates the drape and weight of your vintage fabric. Make style and size assessments to your mock-up and make adjustments to your pattern pieces. This is time-consuming but well worth the effort.

the straight of grain are more likely to be stable. Unless your vintage textile is stable or you plan to stabilize your fabric, be cautious in choosing patterns that are cut on the bias. If you do want to try a bias-cut pattern, hang the vintage textile over your dress form or over a shower curtain rod for a day or two and see what kind of changes occur.

Design Details of the Pattern

Choose a pattern with design details that play up the vintage piece. An asymmetrical front or collar adds an element of surprise to the garment when the period look of a vintage textile is paired with a contemporary design (see the top photo on the facing page). Design details like button loops emphasize the buttons of a garment (see the bottom photo on p. 32).

Fit and Flatter

If a pattern style fits well and looks good, use it over and over. By using a pattern multiple times, you'll fine tune the fit, know the best fabric choices, and develop changes that make the pattern your own. You'll feel confident in the way it looks and feels, and the more times you use it, the easier and faster construction will go, and the better your work is bound to be. With the variety of available vintage fabrics and a little creativity in modifying details and subtly changing the design, no one will ever know you have used the same pattern.

If this is your first attempt with the pattern, work out the bugs first. Determine the size you need and make fitting adjustments as well as desired style changes on the flat pattern. To get a better idea how the adjustments will look, cut the altered pattern out of muslin and make a mock-up. Continue to fine-tune the pattern before cutting into the vintage fabric.

The asymmetrical front design of this blouse pattern accentuates the embroidered corner of the vintage tablecloth. (The Sewing Workshop's Japonesque pattern).

CONSTRUCTION CONSIDERATIONS

Working with vintage textiles may require adjustments in the sewing sequence and techniques you use. Read the pattern instructions again. Think through the order of construction and, to prevent confusion, write any necessary sequence modifications on your pattern instruction sheet and on the pattern piece. If you are adding seam allowances, for instance, don't leave it to chance that you will remember; tape the new seam allowance to the existing pattern or trace a new pattern piece with the additional seam allowance.

This practice will help you in the long term as well as the short term. If you decide to reuse the pattern later with the same modifications, you won't have to rely on your memory (see the top photo on p. 32).

Take the time to experiment with sewing on your vintage textile even if all you can spare are small scraps. If you don't have enough fabric for samples, consider combining the vintage fabric with other fabric rather than skipping this important step. Think about preparatory details such as interfacing and seam finishes, and make samples to determine which are most appropriate. Assess the needle, stitch length, and thread choices you have made by sewing a seam and examining the results. Make necessary changes and note this information on your pattern instruction sheets (see the left photo on p. 33).

Interfacing

With proper interfacing, you can provide structural support to the garment without changing the hand of the fabric. The pattern instructions recommend which pattern pieces will need interfacing, but vintage textiles may be fragile and require additional interfacing to provide extra support in areas like hems and under buttons. Use your judgment and interface wherever the fabric feels fragile, limp, or unstable, or if you are concerned that it won't withstand wear and tear.

Find an interfacing that works well by experimenting on a piece of the vintage fabric. Fusible interfacings are a good choice when compatible with the fabric and

Both the matching color and contrasting shape of the celluloid buttons inspired this blouse design from The Sewing Workshop.

If the garment
you are con-
structing seems
limp, step back
and take another
look. Part of the
beauty of the
vintage textile is
its aged appear-
ance. If you feel
compelled to
bleach, whiten,
iron, and starch,
you'll never be
satisfied with
your creation.
Instead, make
the textile into a
soft nightgown
or pair of comfy
pillowcases.

properly applied. Follow the manufacturer's directions for applying the interfacing, and use a press cloth between the iron and fabric, monitoring heat tolerance closely to avoid damaging the delicate vintage textile.

Traditional sew-in interfacings provide support where fusing is not desirable, as in the case of vintage fabric that has an embroidered surface—the heat and pressure of the iron required for fusible interfacing could flatten and possibly damage the embroidery. A better choice would be a silk organza that would provide support without stiffness. Try tulle as an interfacing for lace to provide support without being obviously visible under the sheer lace.

Whatever type of interfacing you choose, preshrink it first. Sew-in interfacings like silk organza and tulle can be machine-washed (in a lingerie bag if you have a small amount) on gentle cycle, and air-dried or placed in the dryer on low heat. Preshrink fusible interfac-ing by soaking it in warm water at least 30 minutes, avoiding agitation. Then gently squeeze out excess water, and lay it flat on a towel or drape it over a drying rack. While you're at it, preshrink anything else that will go into your garment, such as elastic, zippers, and trim.

Seam Finishes

A seam-allowance finish, such as a serged, zigzagged, or pinked edge, prevents raveling while

The appliqués for this blouse came from faded vintage curtain fabric and were paired with a contemporary fabric and collar design. The simple button loops do not distract from the vintage glass buttons.

Write pattern changes you've made on the pattern pieces as well as on the instruction sheets.

remaining soft and flexible. For the most part seam allowances needed for vintage fabrics are not different from what you usually use in your sewing, so test your favorite seam finish, or use the one recommended in the pattern instructions.

Needle, Stitch Length, and Thread

Ideally, seams should look nearly invisible and without puckers. Consult the needle manufac-turer's suggestions when selecting a needle size, thread, and stitch length that works with your fabric. Experiment with your fabric, be-ginning with a new, size 80/12 universal nee-dle and a 2.5 mm stitch length. Choose a smaller needle and possibly a smaller stitch length when working with fine fabrics. When working with heavier fabrics, such as tapes-tries or wool, use bigger needles and longer stitches.

Select quality threads that are appropriate for the vintage fabric. Mercerized cotton thread has a low sheen with less stretch and strength than polyester thread and is recom-mended for sewing with natural-fiber fabrics.

Polyester thread is a strong thread with some stretch and is recommended for sewing with man-made fabrics and knits. Silk thread is a strong, lustrous thread used for sewing on silk fabrics.

More Samples

You've made samples to determine the best interfacing and seam finishes, and you've made the appropriate needle, thread, and stitch-length choices. The more you experiment with your vintage textile now, the more predictable and to your liking your finished project will be. Try these last few trial runs before you begin construction:

+ Make a few sample seams and examine them. If the fabrics shifted during sewing, one of the fabrics may have stretched. Put the less stable fabric (the fabric that stretches the most), on the bottom. Or use a walking foot in place of your regular sewing machine presser foot to minimize shifting.

+ If the pattern calls for a new or difficult technique, try it on a sample of your vintage fabric.
+ If buttonholes are required, make samples to see how the fabric responds.
+ If you want to try techniques like pintucking or stenciling, now is the time.
+ Using the test sample you created above, wash, dry, and press it using the method you will use for the finished garment. Check for shrinkage and seam puckering, and look for any ill effects from the heat of the iron. Adjust the cleaning and pressing methods as necessary.

NEXT STEPS

Now you are ready to create your own project from vintage fabrics. But before you actually take scissors to cloth, read the next chapter, which walks you through the way I get a project ready to sew. I think you'll find it much easier to develop your own ideas when you've seen the way I worked out one of mine.

When you critique the sample you have made, record the information and keep it close at hand until your project is finished.

Instead of putting buttonholes all down the fragile edge of this top, I put only enough so that I could slip it over my head. The remaining buttons were sewn on, giving the illusion of a traditional opening.

DESIGNER GIFT BAGS

Take the brown paper lunch sack to new heights by using this basic shape in combination with vintage linens to create a gift bag that is as special as the gift inside.

Find an embroidered tea towel and make a bag for a loaf of bread or a bottle of wine to give as a housewarming gift. A white damask tablecloth or an embroidered runner can be used to make a memorable bag for a wedding gift. Whenever possible, use the finished edge of the vintage textile as the top of the bag, and place the embroidered corners and edges of the vintage piece for maximum impact. The instructions that follow are for making a gift bag for a bottle of wine, but you can make yours in any size.

MATERIALS

+ 2 pieces vintage fabric, each 8½ in. wide and 18 in. long
+ 2 pieces narrow cording, each 18 in. long
+ Matching thread
+ Thin cardboard or index card

1. Place the fabric pieces right sides together, and trim edges so they are aligned. Using a ¼-in. seam allowance, sew together, leaving one short edge open. Press seams open.

2. To box the bottom of the bag, work with one corner at a time and fold the bag so a side seam is on top of the bottom seam and the corner lies flat; press. Using a ruler and chalk marker, make a dot 1 in. from the corner point. Draw a line through this dot, perpendicular to the seam. Sew along this line. Cut off the corner triangle, leaving about a ¼-in. seam allowance. Repeat this process on the other side of the bag bottom.

3. Turn the bag right side out. To form the side crease, press a line along the side of the bag, 1½ in. from the side seam. Now form a side crease 1½ in. from the other side of the seamline. Form two more creases on the opposite side of the bag in the same manner.

4. Using an edgestitch foot (or an accurate eye, if you don't have an edgestitch foot), topstitch the creases in place a scant ⅛ in. from the edge. Edgestitch the bottom of the bag in the same manner.

5. To hem the top of the bag, fold ¼ in. toward the wrong side and press, and then fold under another 2½ in. and press. Use your edgestitch foot to stitch the bag hem in

Cut around the damaged portion of a beautiful vintage linen and make this simple gift bag.

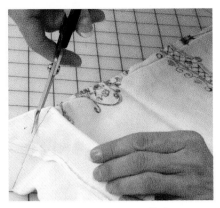

STEP 2 **After sewing, cut off the corner, leaving a ¼ in. seam allowance.**

STEP 3 **Press on each side of each seamline to create side creases.**

STEP 4 **To give the bag form, topstitch ⅛ in. from the edge of each crease.**

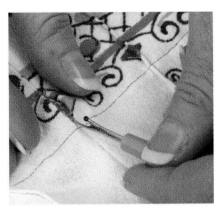

STEP 6 **Using a seam ripper, carefully open up the side seams of the casing by removing 5 or 6 stitches.**

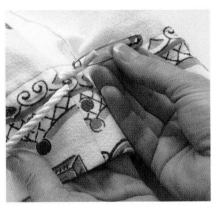

STEP 7 **Use a safety pin to thread the cord through the side opening in the casing and back out again.**

STEP 8 **Knot the cord ends together and pull the bag closed.**

place. Then stitch again ¾ in. from the hem. This will form the casing for the drawstring.

6. To provide an opening for inserting the drawstrings, the two side seams in the casing must be opened up. From the right side of the bag, gently pull the seam apart and carefully insert the blade of a seam ripper, removing five or six stitches. Repeat on the opposite side seam.

7. Beginning at the side seam opening, use a safety pin or bodkin to insert one of the cords through the entire casing, coming out through the same opening. Repeat, threading the remaining cord through the opposite side seam opening in the same way.

8. Knot the cord ends together on each side. Pull on the knots to draw the bag closed.

9. To maintain the shape of the bag, insert a piece of thin cardboard cut to size into the bottom of the bag.

Here are some more creative ideas for your gift bag:

✦ Another way to close the bag is to fold over the bag top and add a button and buttonhole. Or simply skip the drawstring step and tie the bag with ribbon or lace.

✦ Make a larger bag out of an old leather or wool coat; add a handle and you've made a purse.

Binding an Edge

If you don't have enough fabric for a facing, if you want to simplify the neckline, or if you just want to add a design element, modify the pattern by eliminating the facing altogether. Necklines in ready-to-wear are often finished with a strip of bias-cut fabric. This can be done so the bias shows on the outside of the garment or only on the inside, but whichever you choose, the bias strip encases the raw edge, eliminating the need for a shaped facing (see the photo at right). If you want to bind your garment and the main fabric is too

Replacing the neckline finish with bias binding gave this dress a cleaner, more professional look.

By creating a diagonal yoke for the back of this jacket, I was able to squeeze this jacket out of less fabric and make it more interesting at the same time.

heavy, choose something lighter for the bias strip.

I use a variation on the traditional method to create a ⅜-in. bias binding neckline finish that looks good every time. A no-fuss method, it requires only that you do three things accurately: Cut the bias strips 1¾ in. wide, trim the neckline seam allowance to ⅜ in., and topstitch from the right side. Make a test sample first and take a close look at the width of the bias strips. If the fabric used for the bias strip is thick, the strip may need to be wider to accommodate the turn of the cloth. You can use this method to bind any edge—just don't sew the binding into a ring for a straight edge.

To make bias binding for a neckline finish, you will need ⅓ yd. of fabric or more if you do not want to seam the binding.

1. Fold one end of the binding fabric at a 45-degree angle to the selvage, and cut along this bias foldline. Place a ruler along this edge and mark a 1¾-in.-wide strip. If the strip is not at least 1 in. longer than the

For a neater finish when top-stitching a bias binding, turn the fabric and manipulate the fold into the correct position, holding it in place with your fingers. Sew forward and stop every 2 in. to 3 in. to adjust your fingers.

Making Bias Binding

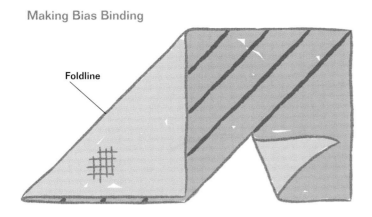

Foldline

neckline, mark a second strip. Cut out the strips (see the illustration above).

2. If you need to piece the strips, place two, right sides together and short ends aligned as shown, and sew. Press the seam open. Repeat if necessary.

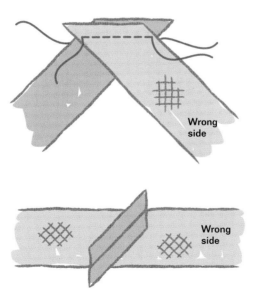

Wrong side

Wrong side

3. Measure the neckline along the seamline. Add ¾ in. to the measurement and cut the bias strip to this length, cutting square, not diagonal, ends. Using a ⅜-in. seam allowance, sew the ends of the strip together to form a ring the same size as the neckline.

4. Trim the neckline seam allowance to ⅜ in. Pin the right side of the neck binding to the wrong side of the neck opening, matching the seamed end of the bias strip to one of the shoulder seams. Stitch in place using a ⅜-in. seam allowance. From the garment wrong side, press the seam allowances and bias binding away from the garment.

Attaching Bias Binding

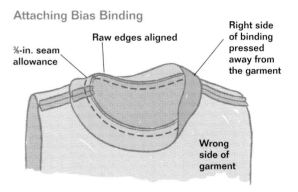

⅜-in. seam allowance

Raw edges aligned

Right side of binding pressed away from the garment

Wrong side of garment

5. Working from the right side of the garment, fold the raw edge of the binding to the middle of the bias strip, so it almost touches the neckline seam allowance.

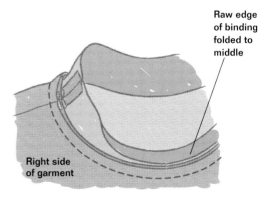

Raw edge of binding folded to middle

Right side of garment

6. Bring the binding foldline down over the stitching line of the neckline, encasing the raw edge. To topstitch the binding in place, position the edgestitch foot along the edge of the neck binding on the garment right side. With the needle over one position to the right, stitch in place. Press. (See the illustration on the facing page.)

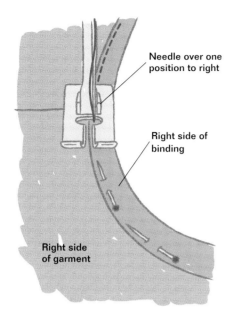

Needle over one
position to right

Right side of
binding

Right side
of garment

Topstitch ⅛ in. from the seamline, on the garment side.

Neckline Finish as a Design Feature

For an attractive and easy variation on a bias binding neckline finish, try this. The result is a binding with a delicate overlap at the center front.

1. Trim the neckline seam allowance to ⅜ in.

2. Cut a bias strip of fabric 1½ in. wide and the circumference of the neck opening plus 1½ in.

3. Folding it with the wrong side in, press the bias band in half lengthwise.

4. Beginning at the center front and aligning the raw edges, pin the right side of the band to the right side of the neckline. When you begin, swing the first end of the band into the neck opening, pin the band to the neckline, and finish by overlapping the last end of the band across the first, then swinging it into the neck opening.

5. Stitch the band to the garment neckline using ⅜-in. seam allowance. Trim the extend-

ing ends of the band at the center front, finish the seam edge, and press the seam toward the garment.

6. Topstitch ⅛ in. from the seamline, on the garment side (see the photo above).

Adding Length with Lace

Here is a way to lengthen a blouse by adding lace around the bottom. You can adapt this method to lengthen a skirt or pants legs.

1. Determine the desired length of the blouse, and draw a line marking the bottom edge on the front and back pattern pieces. Measure the depth of the lace; subtract ¼ in. Draw another line this distance above the "bottom edge" line. Cut off the excess pattern along the second line.

2. Calculate the bottom width of the blouse and measure the yardage of the lace to be sure you have enough. If you have more than you need to go around, consider gathering the lace to fit instead of cutting it. If you do cut the lace, refer to the sidebar on p. 45 for guidance.

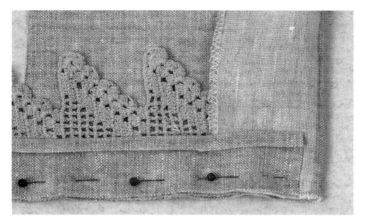

Place the lace against the bottom edge of the blouse, fold the facing back on top, and add the hem facing. Pin in place.

Press the hem facing toward the wrong side of the garment, with the lace extending from the bottom edge, and stitch in place.

If you are short on fabric, add length with a pretty lace edging.

3. When you cut out the blouse, cut a hem facing out of the same or a contrasting fabric, making it 1½ in. wide and long enough to go around the bottom of the blouse. Press under ¼ in. along one long edge.

4. Once the side seams of the blouse are joined and the front facings attached, place the blouse right side up on your work surface, with the facings extended away from the garment. Position the lace right side down along the bottom edge of the blouse, aligning the top edge of the lace with the bottom edge of the blouse and beginning and ending at the front facing seamline. Baste in place.

5. Fold each facing back along its seamline and on top of the lace. Lay the hem facing wrong side up, raw edges even, on top. Pin. (See the top photo at left.)

6. Stitch along the bottom edge of the blouse, using a ¼-in. seam allowance.

7. Turn the bottom front corners right side out, folding the front and hem facings against the wrong side of the blouse so the lace extends from the bottom seam. Press the hem facing toward the wrong side of the garment and hand-stitch in place (see the center photo at left). Turn under the vertical edge of each front facing, and stitch in place.

Combine Fabrics

Combining a vintage textile with other fabrics not only will increase the available yardage, it's bound to make the garment more interesting. You can use new fabric or other vintage pieces, adding one additional fabric or many. Keep in mind the design principles we dis-

STOP UNRAVELING

Lace

To prevent unraveling when you cut through a piece of lace or a knitted sweater, try this:

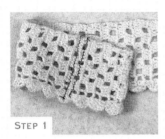

STEP 1

STEP 2

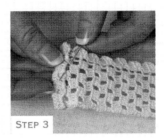

STEP 3

1. Use a straight stitch or a narrow zigzag and stitch two parallel rows ¼ in. apart along the desired cutting line.

2. Cut between the two rows of stitching.

3. Tuck under each cut end, then turn under again and hand-stitch.

Knits and Woolens

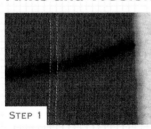

STEP 1

STEP 3

To prevent unraveling when cutting through a loosely woven fabric or a knitted fabric such as a sweater, follow this similar technique:

1. Sew two parallel rows of stitching along the cutting line, and cut between them.

2. Rather than try to turn under the bulky fabric, zigzag or serge each cut edge, taking care not to stretch the fabric.

3. Turn back this finished edge and hand- or machine-stitch in place.

If a small area continues to be at risk for unraveling, use a drop of a fray retardant to prevent the problem.

When deciding on a combination of fabrics, consider textiles with varying textures, and throw in a color that doesn't exactly match.

cussed in chapter 2, and make sure the combination is pleasing to the eye.

Lay out your fabric choices on a neutral background (for instance on a bed or floor covered with a white sheet) and take stock of the situation. Look for a common element, such as color, texture, or type of handwork. Consider a fabric or vintage textile with an interesting texture or perhaps a combination you don't normally pick, such as florals and stripes. If you are using your vintage textile as an accent piece, try a neutral fabric that highlights it as the companion fabric (see the top photo at left).

Once you've made some selections, consider how you will combine them. One way to do this is to use different fabrics for various pattern pieces. You can use different fabrics for facings, collar and cuffs, a blouse yoke, or a vest back (see the bottom photo at left). Make a sketch of your design to help visualize the fabric combinations. Or take it a step further and draw from your days of playing with paper dolls. Using your sketch or enlarged line drawings of the pattern, glue potential fabric choices in place. The scale of the fabric will not be accurate in the sample, but use your imagination to visualize the combinations.

A CHALLENGING EXAMPLE

Now I'm going to walk you through the process I use in making a blouse from a vintage tablecloth. In this section we'll put what we've learned into practice, including selecting a pattern, copying and modifying

Using contrasting fabrics for pattern pieces and facings can be a necessity and also adds interest to a garment.

the pattern, combining fabrics and lace, and laying and cutting out the pattern.

When I found this tablecloth I fell in love with the color and pattern of the flowers and vines (see the photo at right). Repeated washings had given it a slightly faded color and a soft texture, and in my mind, character. I had originally planned to use it for a child's jacket, but when I discovered some beautiful vintage lace at an antiques store I changed my mind. The lace had texture and was similar in color to the tablecloth background, so, knowing I would appreciate it more than my daughter, I decided to combine the two into a garment for myself. Follow along as I go through the step-by-step process that I used, from selecting a pattern to cutting it out.

When I use a tablecloth for a project, I try to include the border pattern in my planning. Some tablecloths have a central design as well as a border along the edges. Whether printed or woven, the design might be figurative with clearly recognizable objects like flowers, fruit, or cherubs, or thematic, as seen in Art Deco tablecloths. The border is sometimes directional, with a definite vertical or horizontal orientation, and in the case of a square or a rectangular tablecloth it could be on two or four sides. All of these characteristics of border tablecloths limit the amount of fabric available by restricting the pattern layout (see the top left photo on p. 48).

Step 1: Selecting a Garment Pattern

I begin by placing the tablecloth over a dress form and standing back for a good look. I can get a three-dimensional idea of what I want, and sketch some ideas (see the bottom photo on p. 48). In this case, my vision was of a box-styled blouse, without details like darts or pleats that would interrupt the surface design of the tablecloth. I chose The Sewing Workshop's Mizono blouse pattern because of its

Putting this tablecloth over the dress form gave it dimension and helped me determine how to position the border design on the garment.

style, and I also liked the idea of an asymmetrical collar for added interest (see the top right photo on p. 48). I decided to add wide crocheted lace to the blouse bottom to soften the square lines.

Step 2: Modifying the Pattern

The changes I made to highlight the vintage tablecloth included:

- ✦ eliminating the lower panel of the front and back to shorten the blouse.
- ✦ combining the individual panels of the front and back. Breaking up the floral pattern of the fabric would have been a design distraction, so the panels were eliminated.

Take advantage of a tablecloth with a border print by incorporating it into the design of a garment.

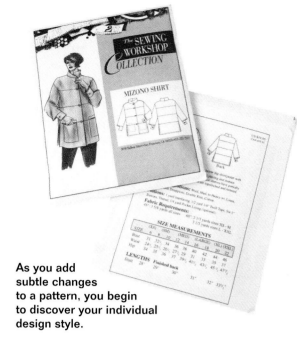

As you add subtle changes to a pattern, you begin to discover your individual design style.

Put pen to paper and sketch your design idea.

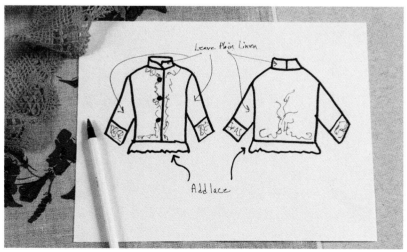

+ reversing the left and right collar pieces so the collar folds over rather than stands up.
+ deleting the cuffs. The separate cuff design of the pattern seemed too formal.
+ creating a separate sleeve facing to make a turn-back out of contrasting fabric. I like

the three-quarter-length sleeves, and the sleeve turn-back was a detail that added interest.

+ cutting the front facings separately from the blouse fronts (due to fabric shortage).
+ adding a hem facing so lace could be added to the blouse hemline.

Step 3: Combining Fabrics

I decided to bring another fabric into the design, partly because the floral tablecloth was only 52 in. by 52 in., but also because I didn't want the entire blouse to be made from the tablecloth. As my daughter once said, "It's okay if you make stuff from tablecloths, Mom, but you don't want to look like one." I tried pairing the floral tablecloth with a red geometrically patterned tablecloth, but decided it made it look too "country" (see the top photo on the facing page).

In the end, I decided to use a plain linen tablecloth of a similar color and texture for the second fabric. I cut only the fronts, back, and sleeve facings from the floral tablecloth and cut the remaining pattern pieces from the plain tablecloth. I thought this combination would emphasize the simple beauty of the floral fabric and lace without overwhelming them.

Step 4: Copying the Pattern

I had used this pattern previously, and size adjustments had been made to the original pattern, including style and pattern changes listed above. I transferred the necessary pattern markings: grainlines, center foldlines, matching notches, etc. (see the bottom photo at right).

Step 5: Laying Out the Pattern

The most scientific thing you do when you sew is lay out the pattern. When faced with a shortage of vintage fabric, you sometimes need to pull in mathematical skills. Be sure to give special attention to the direction of the pattern pieces to avoid upside-down designs. Pattern pieces on which fabric designs must match across seamlines, such as center fronts and sides, need to be strategically placed during pattern layout.

To lay out the pattern, I needed a large space to allow me to place all the pattern pieces down on the fabric at one time. I put two cutting mats on the floor of our basement, put on my garden knee pads and hoped I wouldn't have visitors. (Seriously, it takes awhile, and the knee pads really do help.) I gathered the essentials: ruler, pattern weights, chalk marker, rotary cutter and scissors, pattern pieces, and in this case, the cleaned and pressed tablecloths.

Keeping in mind grainline and matching requirements, the blouse fronts were placed so the flower motifs were along the bottom edge and the center fronts. The back was positioned so the flower motifs were along the bottom edge and down the center back, and the sleeve facings were placed so the flowers ran through their center (see the bottom

When combining fabrics, think about the overall look. To me this was too "country."

photo on p. 50). The rest of the pattern pieces were cut from the plain linen tablecloth.

Step 6: Cutting Out

I transferred markings from the pattern to the fabric. My preference is to use tailor's tacks when sewing with vintage fabrics, but chalk

Reuse your fully adjusted patterns as much as possible. They're tailor-made to you, and your imagination can make each one unique.

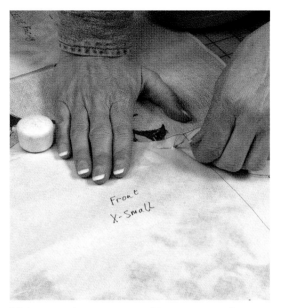

markers, tracing paper, and erasable pens also work as long as you test their disappearing characteristics first. I used pattern weights to secure the pattern pieces, although pins do the same thing, and cut out the pattern pieces, using a rotary cutter (see the photo at left).

This is the thought process and mechanics I use each time to select and modify a pattern and to determine fabric combinations. With planning and flexibility, the pattern layout for the vintage fabric comes together in a creative fashion. Your time on the floor with your knee pads in place is well worth it!

Make sure the pattern markings you use do not damage the vintage fabric.

Move from three-dimensional to two-dimensional. When you place the pattern piece, think about the positioning of the floral design you liked when the tablecloth was on the dress form.

MAKING A SELF-FACED SLEEVE CUFF

A self-faced sleeve rolls up to reveal a cuff out of the same fabric. To create this detail, first decide how long you want the sleeve and how deep you want the self-facing. If your fabric has a right and wrong side, follow the directions for adding a contrasting facing.

Lay a piece of tracing paper over the bottom of the sleeve pattern and trace the shape of the sleeve from the bottom up as far as you wish the facing to go (see the left illustration below). Cut out the tracing, flip it over, abut it with the sleeve end, and tape the pieces together (see the center illustration below). Cut out the sleeve and construct as recommended in your pattern instructions. When the sleeve is hemmed and turned up, it will reveal a cuff out of the same fabric (see the photo at right).

For a sleeve facing made of contrasting fabric, add a seam allowance to the abutting edges of the sleeve-facing pattern and sleeve pattern (see the right illustration below). With right sides together, sew the sleeve facing to the sleeve edge. Press the seam allowance toward the sleeve, and continue construction as recommended in the instructions. When the sleeve is hemmed and turned up, it will reveal a cuff out of contrasting fabric.

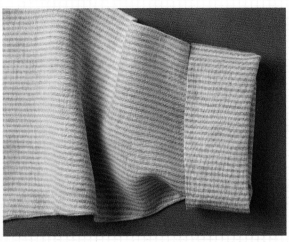

If you like to roll up your sleeves, add a self-faced sleeve detail.

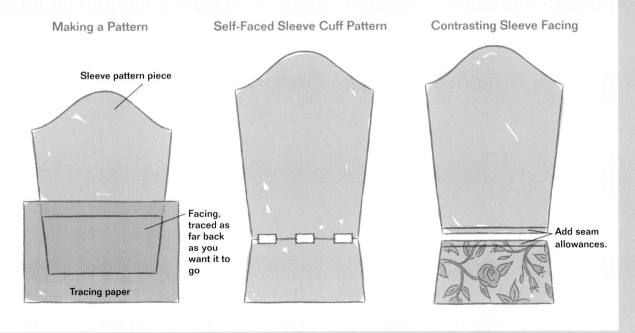

Making a Pattern

Sleeve pattern piece

Tracing paper

Self-Faced Sleeve Cuff Pattern

Facing, traced as far back as you want it to go

Contrasting Sleeve Facing

Add seam allowances.

CHRISTMAS STOCKINGS

Add something old to your holiday decor with the addition of Christmas stockings you've made from vintage textiles and create a one-of-a-kind heirloom. Make several for impact and hang them on your mantel, or spread them around the house—over a chair, on a shelf, on your front door. Here are some fabrics you could consider for making a stocking and cuff:

+ *an old wool sweater that has been washed and dried so it is full and soft*
+ *vintage tablecloths such as a white damask or a colorful '50s-style fabric*
+ *embroidered tea towels*
+ *vintage blankets, bedspreads, and old quilts*

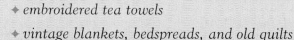

Combine reverse appliqué with traditional appliqué, and use a pinked rotary blade to give the cut edges of the wool stocking interest.

MATERIALS

+ *Vintage textiles and trims*
+ *Lining fabric*
+ *Quilt batting or cotton flannel*
+ *Ribbon, cording, or fabric for hanging loop*

1. Draw a stocking pattern on paper. Have fun with it. Make the pattern large or small, long and narrow, elf-like with toes that curl up, or wide and oversized to hold lots of goodies. For a cuff pattern, draw a band twice the width of the top of the stocking pattern and any depth you want. Add a ¾-in. seam allowance around both patterns. If you aren't having luck with drawing your own pattern, buy one. I hate those patterns that say "1 square = 1 in.," so I won't present one here. Life is too short.

2. Cut a stocking front and back from your desired fabric (remember to turn the pattern over for the back). Cut one cuff from the same or a different fabric (omit the bottom seam allowance to take advantage of a decorative edge on your fabric). Cut a stocking front and back from lining fabric. If you want a soft, lofty look, cut a front and back the same size from quilt batting, or for a little less puff, from flannel.

3. Taking your cues from ideas we've discussed, embellish the front of the stocking (and the back if desired) or just the cuff.

4. Stack the cut-out pieces in the following order, and then pin the layers together in the following order:

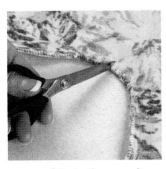

STEP 6 **Clip to the seamline on the inside curves of the stocking to help it lay flat when turned to the right side.**

STEP 7 **Slip your hand between the lining layers and turn the stocking so the lining is on the outside.**

STEP 8 **Overlap the ends of the cuff at the stocking seam allowance and stitch, using a ¾-in. seam allowance.**

STEP 9 **When the stocking is turned to the right side, the cuff will flip over the top of the stocking, covering the seam allowance.**

+ stocking front and back, right sides together
+ one layer of batting
+ the front and back lining pieces right sides together
+ the remaining batting

5. Turn the stacked fabrics so the stocking fabric is on top.

6. Using a ¾-in. seam allowance and leaving the top open, sew the layers together along the edges. Finish the seam allowance edge if desired. Clip the inside curves.

7. Slip your hand between the lining layers and turn the stocking so the lining is on the outside.

8. Hem the cuff along the sides and bottom or use the existing decorative edge from the vintage textile. Lay the cuff (do not seam the ends together) over the stocking, with the right side of the cuff against the lining side of the stocking. Overlap the cuff ends at the back seam of the stocking. Pin in place, then stitch, using a ¾-in. seam allowance.

9. Slip your hand inside the stocking and turn it right side out, flipping the cuff over the stocking top.

10. To hang the stocking, attach a length of cording, ribbon, or fabric at the top of the back. Topstitch in place. Add buttons or beads if you like.

Here are some ideas to get you started on making wonderful, creative stockings:

+ Use the appliqué techniques described on pp. 62–67 to create a design on your stocking front before assembling. See the photo on the facing page.
+ Keep the body of the stocking simple and add a decorative cuff. Use an embroidered towel or the fringe from a hand towel for the cuff. Or assemble the body of the stocking and cuff out of the same fabric and embellish with buttons, beads, fringe, or whatever you like. Combine vintage tablecloths and embellish with lace.
+ Make the body of the stocking from an old wool coat or suit and create a cuff from a fur collar. Or combine a fur cuff with a glitzy new fabric.

+ Find an old, lace-embellished pillowcase and use the lace to embellish a stocking cuff. One pillowcase usually has enough lace for two stockings.
+ Use the capabilities of your sewing or embroidery machine to monogram the stocking cuff.
+ Use vintage napkins or an embroidered tablecloth edge as the cuff of a stocking.
+ Fell an old sweater and combine it with wool fabrics to create a fun stocking. See the photo below.

Cut apart an old sweater or coat and wash the fabric to create unusual and fun Christmas stockings.

CHAPTER FOUR

EMBELLISHING VINTAGE TEXTILES

Vintage textiles are often lovely in their own right. So when you've got a beautiful vintage textile, why change it?

Actually, there are many reasons—some practical and others just fun. It may be that only a small amount of the vintage piece you have is undamaged, and by combining it with other textiles, altering the surface design, or adding color or pattern, you can enhance the design impact. You can change or manipulate a vintage textile to hide stains, holes, or other problems, or you can tweak the piece to let you express your creativity. You can use techniques as simple as sewing two pieces of fabric together or as elaborate as dyeing and beading to enhance the effect. Several of my favorite techniques are explained here.

PIECING

Sewing fabrics together is what we do to make garments and other items, and vintage textiles are just another resource for doing this. You don't have to be an artist to make a pleasing combination. Use the vintage pieces you really love, but consider adding a few that aren't your favorites. If you expand your repertoire and add a color or a textural combination you don't usually like, you might be surprised at the outcome—the final product could become more interesting and you may have a new appreciation for a piece that you weren't at first drawn to.

An easy way to combine textiles is to piece together squares of fabric from kimonos, embroidered linens, tablecloths, sweaters, ties, or just about any vintage textile. Find a pattern with a rectangular piece—a band on a vest, for example—and make the band out of squares of vintage fabric (see the photo below).

SHEER OVERLAY

Group small pieces of leftover fabric by color. For this vest, I pieced purple fabrics with kimono fabrics to make the vest's band.

Perhaps you have a beautiful vintage textile you'd like to use, but it is delicate, scratchy to the touch, or damaged. With the addition of a sheer overlay on the piece, you can incorporate it into your design. Use sheer fabrics such as silk or polyester

If you want to use a fragile textile for a collar piece, protect it with a layer of organza. To protect the fragile piece from laundering, make the collar removable.

chiffon, silk organza, or tulle to cover the vintage piece. Besides providing protection, these sheer fabrics can soften the texture and, depending on the color you choose, can mute or change the color. To create a sheer overlay for a collar, for example, cut the collar piece from the vintage fabric and the sheer fabric. Baste the two fabrics together and use as one (see the photo above).

Making a Sheer Pillow Cover

If you have a beautiful vintage textile you'd like to make into a pillow but worry it's too fragile, go ahead and make the pillow, but also cover it with a sheer overlay, using the following method:

MATERIALS

- ✦ *Vintage textile pillow, 16 in. sq.*
- ✦ *½ yd. sheer fabric*
- ✦ *2⅔ yd. ribbon of your choice*

1. Prewash, dry, and iron the sheer fabric. Measure the length and width of your vintage pillow (see the bottom photo on the facing page). Cut two pieces of sheer fabric, 2 in. wider and 4 in. longer than the pillow to allow for hems, seam allowances, and ease.

TRY THIS

+ Collect handkerchiefs or old flour sacks. Piece them together to make a duvet cover.

+ Gather together embroidered pieces and cut same-width pieces of random lengths. Join the rectangles together end to end to make several lengths. Sew the strips together on their length-wise edges until you get a desired width. Use this newly constructed piece of fabric for a vest front, pocket, or collar. Or use it in a home-decorating proj-ect to make a pillow or table runner.

This quilt top, made from vintage flour sacks pieced together, was paired with a dyed tablecloth and made into a duvet cover.

2. To use French seams for construction, place the rectangles of sheer fabric wrong sides together. Using a ⅜-in. seam allowance, sew long sides together. Trim the seam allow-ance to ⅛ in. Turn the rectangle wrong sides out, and stitch ¼ in. from the seam. (see the illustration on p. 58). Press both seam allow-ances toward the back of the pillow cover.

3. To hem the ends of the rectangle, turn the raw edges under 1 in., then turn them under another 1 in. Press, pin, and topstitch in place.

4. For ties, cut eight pieces of ribbon, each 8 in. long. Pin two evenly spaced ribbons to the inside of each end of each rectangle, let-ting the ties extend beyond the rectangle ends. Stitch each tie 1 in. from the pillow edge, on the previous stitching line.

5. Slip the pillow into the sheer case and tie the ribbon closures (see the photo on p. 58).

To determine the size of the sheer pillowcase, measure the length and width of your vintage pillow.

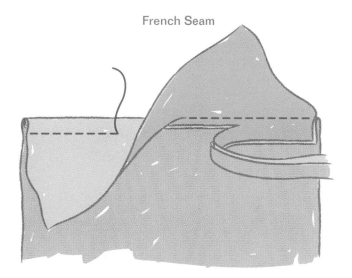

French Seam

TRY THIS

✦ Use similar but mismatched embroidered napkins for the cuffs and collar of a blouse and a sheer overlay to unite them.

✦ Use sheer fabric over a vintage scarf or embroidered piece and make a dressy purse or pillow top.

✦ Slide an old blanket or a fragile quilt into a large chiffon case for a change of appearance and softer texture, as well as a protective cover. Sew a rectangular case large enough to hold the blanket or quilt, leaving one short end open. Hem the open end, add ribbon to tie it closed, and insert the blanket.

The completed pillow slipcover protects the pillow and changes or mutes the color.

CORDED PIPING

This decorative detail is used in garment sewing, as seen on pockets and collar edges, and in home decorating, as on pillows, window treatments, and slipcovers. Vintage men's ties, which are cut on the bias, are an obvious choice for making piping. Other vintage fabrics, while not so obvious, are also good choices: An embroidered dresser scarf, a geometrically patterned tablecloth, and a quilt top are all interesting possibilities. Even a badly stained vintage fabric can work as piping, because the stains tend to disappear as the fabric folds.

To see what your vintage textile would look like as piping, fold it back on itself at a 45-degree angle and cover up all but a ½-in. strip (see the top photo on the facing page). Try your hand at making corded piping using these guidelines.

Making a Sample of Corded Piping

MATERIALS
+ *Minimum ¼ yd. vintage fabric for covering cord*
+ *Minimum 1 yd. rattail, nylon drapery cord, or cotton cable, in desired width*
+ *Zipper foot, cording foot, or pintuck foot*

Rattail, a rounded rayon cord, is a good choice if the project will be dry-cleaned. This cord is flexible, has more body than other cords, and will not crush. If you plan on washing the finished project, however, choose cotton or polyester cord and be sure to preshrink the vintage fabric and cord. To preshrink the cord, place it in a sock, tie the end shut, and add it to a load of laundry.

1. Using the method described on p. 42, cut and sew together enough bias strips to get the desired length. Cut the strips wide enough to wrap around the cord, plus two seam allowances.

2. Lay the cord along the center of the wrong side of the bias strip; fold the fabric in half lengthwise, aligning the raw edges and enclosing the cord.

Use bias-cut fabric to ensure your bindings and pipings are flexible and can be neatly applied. To see how a piping or bias binding will look, fold the fabric back on itself at a 45-degree angle.

3. Attach an accessory foot to the machine: For a zipper foot, set the needle position one place to the left. Sew the bias along the cord, using the left edge of the zipper foot as a guide (see the photo at left and the illustration below). For a cording or pintuck foot, set the needle position to the far right and position the cord under the center groove of the foot; sew.

A zipper foot, pintuck foot, or cording foot can each be used to make piping.

Corded Piping

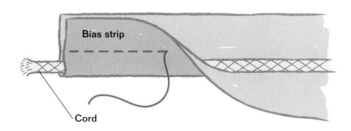

Bias strip

Cord

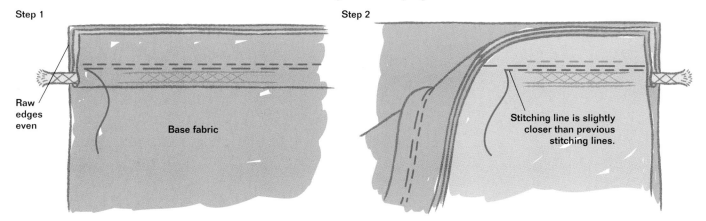

Step 1

Raw edges even

Base fabric

Step 2

Stitching line is slightly closer than previous stitching lines.

Attaching Corded Piping

Piping is typically sandwiched in the seam between adjacent pieces or between a facing and outer piece.

1. Choose an inconspicuous place on the garment to start the piping; for example, under the arm or at a side seam. Lay the piping on top of the right side of the base fabric, aligning the raw edges. Pin in place

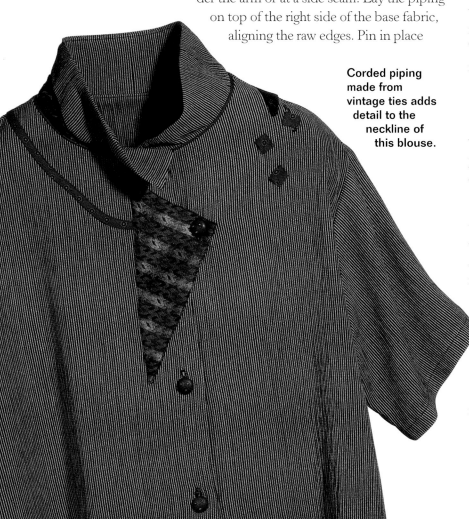

Corded piping made from vintage ties adds detail to the neckline of this blouse.

and baste along the previous stitching line of the piping (see the left illustration above).

2. With right sides together, place the second fabric or facing on top of the piping and base fabric. Flip the work over and pin in place. By turning the work over, you can see the previous stitching line. Set the needle to the far left for the zipper foot or to the half-right position for the cording or pintuck foot. The goal is to stitch slightly closer to the cording and to the left of the previous stitching line (see the right illustration above).

3. Fold the top fabric back along the seam or turn the facing under to reveal the piping, and press. If you have used a nylon or polyester cord, don't let the heat of the iron melt it.

LACE

A renewed interest in nostalgia makes for a more romantic lifestyle and has allowed vintage lace to adorn our homes and apparel. Fortunately, vintage lace is still in abundant supply. You may find several yards rolled into a ball, or a smaller piece attached to a damaged dresser scarf, pillowcase, or collar. Crocheted, tatted, knitted, or machine-made, it comes in many types.

Whatever type of lace you've found, recycle it into your next project.

Removing Lace

If the lace you find is attached to another fabric, look at it carefully to see how it was attached. Was the lace made first (as in crocheted, knitted, and tatted laces) and then stitched to the fabric, or was it worked directly onto the fabric edge?

If it was constructed separately and then stitched to the fabric, use sharp scissors to remove the basting stitches from the wrong

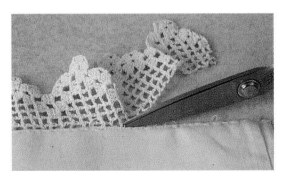

Bring the light source close to safely remove the lace from the fabric edge.

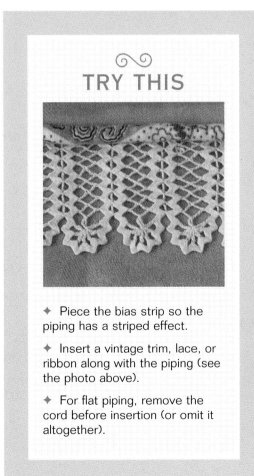

TRY THIS

✦ Piece the bias strip so the piping has a striped effect.

✦ Insert a vintage trim, lace, or ribbon along with the piping (see the photo above).

✦ For flat piping, remove the cord before insertion (or omit it altogether).

If corded piping is used in a straight seam or hem, the fabric that will cover the cord can be cut on the lengthwise or crosswise grain. Because of their inherent stretch, knits, leather, and suede can be cut on the crosswise grain whether the piping is used in a straight or curved seam or hem.

When in doubt of how the lace is attached, cut the lace away and leave a seam.

I cut tubes from fabric cut from an old green velvet prom dress and sewed them to the surface of this vest.

CREATING TEXTURE AND DIMENSION

Texture and dimension provide another enhancement for both vintage and new textiles. We not only need to see things we find enjoyable, we need to touch them as well; if you're like me, the first thing you do when you see a luscious piece of fabric is touch it. If texture and dimension are missing from your vintage textile or you want more, try some of the following techniques. And if your vintage textile is damaged, you can use these techniques to disguise the problem and add a textural element at the same time.

Traditional Appliqué

In traditional or overlay appliqué, fabric shapes are fused and stitched onto a background fabric. Use your vintage fabric as the appliqué, as the background fabric, or both. For the appliqué design, cut out a motif from your vintage piece, draw your own design, or take a design from one of the many crafts or graphic-design books on the market. This method is quick and easy, and works best with light- to medium-weight fabrics that can withstand heat fusing. To use vintage fabric as appliqué fabric, follow these guidelines.

Cutting and Fusing an Appliqué

Choose a design that has simple, graphic lines so it will be possible to sew around the appliqué design.

1. If you are designing your own or are taking the design from a book, create a template. First, trace the design onto paper or make a photocopy, adjusting the size of the image as desired. To avoid distortion of the pattern from a flimsy paper template, trace the tem-

side, where the stitches can be easier to see. Use good light, and before starting, check the basting stitches along the length of the lace to be sure you can find all the stitches (see the bottom photo on p. 61). If the lace is attached directly to the fabric, the easiest removal method I have found is to just cut the lace away from the vintage piece, leaving a seam-allowance width of fabric attached (see the photo above).

Attaching Lace to Your Project

To attach lace that has a seam allowance, insert it in a seam as you would piping (see p. 60). Lace removed from the base fabric (without a seam allowance) can be hand- or machine-stitched onto another fabric or onto the edge of a finished project. The goal is to attach the lace in an inconspicuous manner, so if hand-stitching, use matching thread and small stitches. If you are attaching by machine, use matching or invisible thread, and be careful not to get the presser foot caught in the lace.

✦ Sew lace to the hem of a blouse or sleeve, or to the edge of a cuff or collar.

✦ Use laces on pillows: down the front, around the edges, layered in a random pattern across the pillow top, or combined with other vintage fabrics, trims, and ribbons.

✦ Dye the lace. Try tea dyeing (see p. 17) or use a commercial dye in the washing machine. Add other vintage textiles and use them all together in a project.

✦ Hang a pendant from a length of flat lace, tie the end, and wear it as a necklace (see the photo at left).

✦ Attach lace to a ready-to-wear denim jacket or a linen blouse.

✦ Use lace to embellish a slipcover.

If fusible webbing makes your appliqué too stiff or if the fabric is too delicate to tolerate fusing, try applying it with a fabric spray adhesive, available at any fabric or crafts store. Without the fusible backing, however, the appliqué is more flexible, so be careful not to distort it.

plate onto heavier stock such as tag board or a file folder (see the left photo below).

2. Fuse lightweight fusible webbing to the wrong side of the appliqué fabrics according to the manufacturer's instructions.

3. If you are using a vintage fabric motif, such as a flower, cut out the motif, then remove the paper backing from the fusible webbing. If you are using a template, place the fabric wrong side (paper side) up, then place

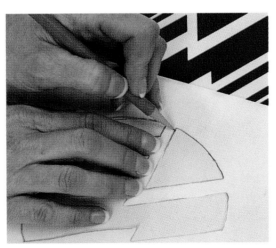

Photocopy or trace an appliqué, then transfer the tracing onto heavier paper, such as a file folder, to prevent distortion when cutting out the pattern.

Iron fusible webbing to the appliqué fabric. Cut out a design in the fabric or draw around a template and cut out the appliqué shape.

the template wrong side up. To make a reverse image, place the template right side up. Trace around the template, cut out the shape, and remove the paper backing (see the right photo on p. 63).

4. Cut out garment pattern pieces according to pattern instructions, or if you are working on a home-decor item, cut out the pieces according to your measurements and design.

5. It is easiest to apply appliqués to a flat surface, so sew just the shoulder or side seams together. If you want to create an uninterrupted flow of the appliqué design, this gives you the option of wrapping it.

6. Check the arrangement of the appliqué pieces by pinning them into place on the pattern piece or garment fabric. Check that the design works in three dimensions by placing the pattern piece on a dress form, or

To get a quick idea of how an appliqué design works in three dimensions, pin the garment fabric over a dress form and then play with the positioning of the appliqué.

placing home-decor projects over a chair or sofa. Stand back and determine if you like what you see. Move the appliqué pieces around until you get a pleasing arrangement (see the photo above).

7. Once you've determined placement, put the appliqués fusible-side down onto the right side of the fabric. Fuse following the manufacturer's instructions.

To add interest to this vest, I appliquéd kimono fabrics to the back, using a design taken from an art-deco scrap-art book.

If you don't want the wrong side of the reverse appliqué on a garment to show, add a lightweight backing fabric to the needlepoint and zigzag the edges together prior to sewing it to the base fabric; or you can line the garment.

Sewing On an Appliqué

1. Position a piece of tear-away stabilizer slightly larger than the appliqué design under the base fabric, and pin in place.

2. Select the zigzag mode on your sewing machine, or use one of your sewing machine's decorative stitches. Set stitch length at 1.5 mm and stitch width at 2 mm as a starting point. Fuse a sample to a scrap of the base fabric to test the machine settings; adjust the stitch length and width to your liking. Once you have determined the settings, position the raw edge of the appliqué fabric under the center of the embroidery or zigzag foot and sew around the edge of the appliqué (see the photo at right).

3. Remove the tear-away stabilizer.

Experiment with your machine's decorative stitches, or if it is more in keeping with the rest of the garment or project to have a slightly frayed edge on the appliqué, use a wider and looser zigzag stitch. If the shape of the appliqué you are sewing is very irregular, sewing with a straight stitch will make it easier to follow the margins.

Reverse Appliqué

In reverse appliqué, two or more layers of fabric are stacked on top of one another and a shape or design is cut out of the upper layer, revealing the layer underneath. In some reverse appliqué, the edges of the resulting "window" are turned under and hemmed to the layer beneath. A simplified version of this technique can be used when wool meltons, felted wool, or Polarfleece are the top fabric. Because these materials do not ravel, the edges of the cut-out shapes do not need to be turned under. Follow along as I describe the method I use to incorporate a vintage needlepoint into the design of a felted wool vest.

Position the raw edge of the fabric under the zigzag or embroidery foot, and sew around the margins of the appliqué.

Making Reverse Appliqué in Wool

Wool needlepoint pieces tend to be stiff and relatively heavy, so pair them with fabrics with comparable characteristics, like upholstery fabric, heavyweight denim, or the wool melton used in this example.

Pick a pattern style that does not require drape and orient the needlepoint for maximum impact, without pointing out the flaws of the piece. In the vest shown on p. 66, I originally tried placing the needle-

The needlepoint piece used for this inset was cut from an unfinished, vertical wall hanging found at an estate sale.

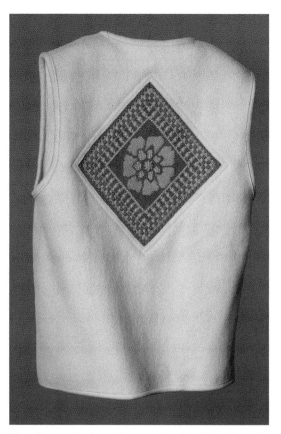

The diagonal orientation masks the distortion of this needlepoint piece.

point square so the sides were perpendicular to the vest hem. This didn't work because of the distortion of the needlepoint. By changing the needlepoint to a diagonal orientation in the center back, the piece has visual impact without drawing attention to the distortion and asymmetry. You can use the entire needlepoint piece for the appliqué or cut it down (see the bottom photo on p. 65).

1. To finish the needlepoint edges, stitch around the piece close to the last rows of needlepoint stitches with a zigzag stitch, and trim away the excess canvas, leaving a ⅜-in. seam allowance. If you want to cut the needlepoint down to a different size or shape, draw the desired outline plus ¾ in. on the wrong side with a chalk marker, and sew over the line with a zigzag stitch, making sure the stitches are close enough together to prevent raveling. Cut out the shape just outside the zigzag stitch (see the photo below).

2. Determine where you want the needlepoint appliqué to go, and chalk the placement marks on the wrong side of the fabric.

3. Position the appliqué on top of the markings, right side down against the wrong side of the vest, and pin in place.

TRY THIS

+ Embellish the front of a jacket or blouse with appliqué pieces taken from a vintage tablecloth or fabric.

+ Cut out embroidered areas from napkins or tablecloths, and appliqué them to panels of fabric to be used in window treatments.

+ To simplify the appliqué process when appliquéing irregular shapes, sew them down with a straight stitch.

To prevent raveling, zigzag around the margins of the desired shape.

4. Stitch ⅜ in. inside the finished edge of the needlepoint, then add a second line of stitching ½ in. inside the first (see the top photo at right). Trim the canvas close to the first line of stitching.

5. With the right side of the vest up, carefully cut away the fabric inside the first stitching line, revealing the needlepoint appliqué (see the center photo at right).

6. Continue with regular construction.

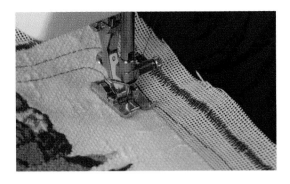

Add a second row of stitching around the reverse appliqué for emphasis.

Carefully cut away the fabric inside the first stitching line to reveal the appliqué underneath it.

BLOCKING VINTAGE NEEDLEPOINT

Most of the wool needlepoint pieces I find are stretched or distorted and no longer on the straight of grain. They can be used as is or the pieces can be blocked, which is done by wetting and stretching the canvas to bring it into better alignment.

Many books describe blocking, but one technique is to spray lukewarm water onto the needlepoint until wet but not saturated. Then stretch it over a towel-covered corkboard or an artist's canvas, anchoring it with T-pins at evenly spaced intervals, and allow it to dry.

Blocking does not always straighten the piece, however, so if you are still left with a distorted needlepoint, consider this a design feature, and position it so the distortion or asymmetry looks deliberate.

When I finished this vest made from new and recycled wools, it needed something. Beading areas of the appliqué gave it a little sparkle and dimension.

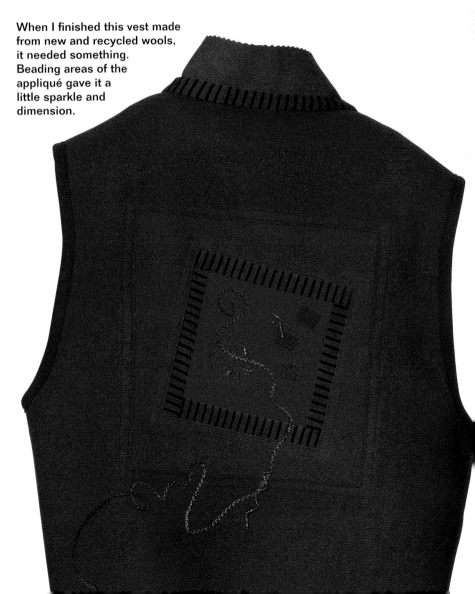

A bead-embellished silk scarf was combined with silk dupioni to make this pillow. The beaded silver scarf serves as a table runner or shawl, depending on the occasion.

Bead Embellishment

I love the look of bead-embellished fabrics and have wanted to add this skill to my repertoire for a long time. A few years ago I took a workshop on tambour beading. The instructor said we would all be producing beaded motifs, bands, and overall designs by the end of the workshop. And indeed, by the end of the second day most of the students had their netted frames full of lovely designs. Not me. I had six beads on my netting. Despite the teacher's patient help, I just couldn't get it. So when my sister suggested I bead a silk damask piano scarf, I said, "Show me." Using simple bead-embroidery techniques, it was possible to highlight the subtle color changes while adding texture to the scarf. If you, too, are beading-challenged, try following these instructions.

Before you begin Clean the vintage fabric prior to beading. If you use washable fabric, you will be able to hand-wash the piece after beading. If the fabric must be dry-cleaned, get to know your dry cleaner, and make sure he or she is familiar with cleaning beaded fabrics. After the fabric is beaded, clean only as often as necessary.

The fabric you intend to embellish needs to be in good shape to withstand the extra weight of the beads as well as the extra handling required for bead application. If you plan on assembling the beaded fabric into a pillow top, garment, or other project, cut out the pattern pieces before beading, interface the pattern pieces to improve the fabric strength and longevity, and when applying the beads avoid areas where the fabric has deteriorated.

Choosing beads Choose beads that enhance your vintage fabric. Use size 11 delicas, Czech or Japanese seed beads, or vintage seed beads. If you use bugle beads, check the edges and discard broken or sharp beads; they will cut through the thread. As a guide, 50 grams of beads in assorted colors were purchased for the 10 in. by 15 in. design in the example on the facing page.

To choose colors, lay out the beads in natural light, heaping them in small piles across the fabric. Look at the color, shape, size, and luster, as well as the reflective surface. String strands of seven or eight beads in various colors on a needle and lay them across your fabric to determine what you like. Choose colors that highlight the design or fabric, and take into consideration the luster of the beads as well. Silk fabric reflects light and is complemented by beads with a shiny surface or a silver lining, while some cottons may look better with beads with a matte or dull finish. These steps take a little time but are well worth the effort to get the look you desire.

In my example, I used colors that highlighted the damask design and chose beads that were shiny and reflected light, in keeping with the silk fabric. The effect the beads have is strong, even stronger than embroidering with silk floss. If their color is complementary, they pop out, creating dimension and texture. If you choose a strong, contrasting color, the effect might overwhelm your fabric; you'll know when you string them across your fabric. If you want a strong contrast, then use beads with bold colors and contrasting finishes. Mix shiny beads with dull ones for dimension, because while shiny beads pop to the forefront of the design, beads with dull finishes retreat into the background.

Beading equipment One thread I use with bead embroidery is Nymo. It is a prestretched nylon thread that is soft enough to use with vintage fabrics and won't fray or break as cotton thread often does. I usually use size D, matching the colors to the fabric and beads.

Check to make sure the needle will go through the hole in the beads. Once you are sure the needles will work, thread several to speed up the embellishment process.

Before you start, give the thread a tug so it won't stretch out later.

Use size 10 to 12 needles when working with Nymo D. Size 10 is best because it is easier to thread, but if your bead holes are uneven or small, use the smaller size 12 needle. If you are using tiny beads—size 12 to 15— use a smaller needle, size 13 to 16, and smaller

Use beads that bring life to the vintage textile.

Use a ring frame or embroidery hoop to stabilize the fabric for beading, but be careful not to crush the glass beads as you change its position.

thread, Nymo B. Keep several needles threaded and ready to use to speed up the bead-embellishment process.

Use a ring frame (also known as an embroidery hoop) larger than your design to keep the fabric taut. Pressure from the embroidery hoop can break glass beads, so plan out the sections to be beaded so the hoop won't need to be placed over previously beaded sections.

Simple Bead Embroidery

Bead embellishment should enhance rather than overwhelm the vintage fabric. Letting the fabric pattern, color, and the beads be your guide, choose a simple pattern, and remember that you don't have to fill in all the areas—often the fabric will suggest the design: Follow the outlines of the flowers or the swirls on the

vintage fabric (see the photos at left and on p. 68). On plain fabric use a tracing pencil and draw a design, taking inspiration from embroidery books and ethnic patterns. Swirls are easier to bead than angles.

If your plan is to assemble the beaded fabric into a garment or home-decor project, be certain you stay well away from seams and cutting lines. In my example, I outlined areas and filled in some motifs using a backstitch. This can be accomplished through the following steps:

MATERIALS

+ *Beads: size 11 delica or seed beads, or bugle beads*
+ *Beading needles or sharps: size 10 or 12*
+ *Nymo thread: size D*
+ *Ring frame (embroidery hoop)*

1. Pour the beads into small saucers, separating them by color.

2. Put the ring frame around the area to be beaded (see the photo above).

Beading

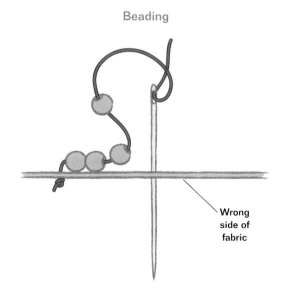

Wrong side of fabric

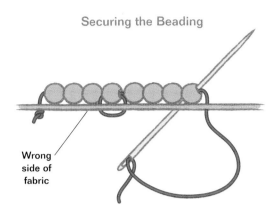

Wrong side of fabric

3. Thread a needle with approximately 1 yd. single thread and knot it, giving it a good tug to stretch the thread.

4. Starting from the wrong side of the fabric, bring the needle up through the right side of the fabric. Scoop up 3 or 4 beads of the desired color onto the needle, slide them down the thread, and align them on the fabric. Pass the needle to the wrong side of the fabric close to the last bead (see the illustration on the facing page).

5. Come back to the right side of the fabric between the last 2 beads placed down. Go through the last bead a second time. This secures all 3 or 4 beads (see the illustration above).

6. Pick up 3 or 4 more beads, lay them down on the fabric as before, and continue in the same manner.

7. To stabilize entire sections of the beads, return the needle to the wrong side, then come up on the right side. Go through the beads another time, following the original path. Try to cover the area of your design with beads, bearing in mind the movement of the pattern.

8. Knot the thread on the wrong side, and cut the excess ¼ in. beyond the knot. The ends will end up on the wrong side.

Don't pull the thread too tightly or the fabric will pucker. If you are having difficulty getting through a bead on the first pass, discard the bead. If you can't get the needle through a bead on the second pass, don't force the needle. Just tack down the thread holding the bead by passing the needle between the two beads and over the thread, thus securing the thread. Don't split threads when going through a second time because this will weaken the thread.

Give this simple bead-embroidery technique a try. Once you've mastered it (you'll find it easy!), try beaded fringe. There are many books that explain this technique, as well as other beading techniques that enhance vintage textiles (see the photo above).

Keep your eyes out for unfinished needlepoint pieces and turn them into purses. Embellish with vintage buttons and beaded fringe.

TRY THIS

✦ By all means, use vintage beaded fabric, but remember it is relatively delicate and may not do well in heavy use or if it needs frequent laundering.

✦ Drape a beaded vintage scarf over a piano, or use it as a table runner.

✦ Frame beaded fabric and hang it on a wall; be aware that the fabric may deteriorate from exposure to sunlight, temperature changes, and the weight of the beads. To minimize damage, back the beaded piece with a heavier fabric before beading.

✦ Incorporate vintage fabrics you have beaded into the design of a garment, for example a lapel.

✦ Add a small amount of beading to highlight a vintage pieced appliqué.

✦ Turn beaded vintage fabric into a pillow top.

✦ Make a purse out of a bead-embellished fabric.

Pieced kimono fabrics embellished with beads are appliquéd to this jumper.

Corded pintucks were used on this linen pillow to give the flap stability and weight.

Corded Pintucks

One my favorite ways to create dimension and texture using sewing-machine stitches is to sew corded pintucks. A double needle is used in conjunction with a pintuck presser foot. The presser foot is designed to ride over a narrow cord, creating small ridges in the fabric. Different sizes of pintuck feet and double needles are available for different fabric weights, so check your sewing-machine instruction guide. Use a thin cord, preshrunk and colorfast, such as pearl cotton thread.

Creating Corded Pintucks

MATERIALS

✦ *Fabric for project*
✦ *Pintuck foot*
✦ *Double needle*
✦ *Cotton embroidery thread*
✦ *Pearl cotton thread*

1. Cut the fabric larger than needed for the pattern piece, and cut it to size when you've finished pintucking. With the right side of the fabric up, baste a line of stitching (straight or in a curved design) to act as a guide for the first row of stitching.

2. For fine- to medium-weight fabrics, use a 5- to 7-groove pintuck foot and a 2.0/90 twin needle. Use cotton embroidery thread, and set the sewing machine for a 2 mm-long straight stitch. Remove the needle plate and thread the cord through the hole, then reattach the needle plate (see the top photo at right).

To make corded pintucks, a narrow cord is threaded through the hole in the needleplate of the sewing machine, then sewn overusing a double needle.

Pintucks can be used to hide small stains or flaws in vintage fabric, and at the same time create interesting texture and dimension.

TRY THIS

The stained area in the center linen piece of this pillow was camouflaged with pintucks and a vintage shoe buckle.

✦ Use a decorative stitch between rows of pintucks for a different look.

✦ Use horizontal pintucks 2 in. above the hem of a dress to give body and dimension.

✦ Use pintucks to disguise a damaged embroidered linen. If you don't have enough fabric, combine new fabric embellished with pintucks (see the photo above).

3. Place the fabric under the presser foot, aligning the basting line over the cord. Sew the first tuck along the basting line. When you reach the end of the fabric, turn and place the first tuck under one of the grooves of the foot, and sew the second row. Continue in this way until finished (see the bottom photo above).

COLOR

Whether your goal is to create your own fabric design, enhance the weave of the fabric, provide cohesion to a group of fabrics, or just cover a stain, adding color to a vintage textile is another way to express your creativity.

Fabric Paints

Acrylic fabric paints are used in stenciling and stamping. There are several choices: transparent, semitransparent, and opaque. They can be metallic, pearlescent, fluorescent, and even glow-in-the-dark. They are easy to use—no special equipment or chemicals is required—and generally require heat-setting when dry. Best of all, they come in a variety of colors that can be blended and mixed to achieve desired effects.

The first time I added color to a vintage fabric was out of necessity. The tablecloth was exactly the color and texture I wanted, but the stains made it unusable, or so I thought. I found that stenciling fabric paint in an allover, random pattern covered the stains effectively.

Follow these simple guidelines to stencil or stamp your vintage textile. Be sure to experiment on scrap fabric until you get the hang of it.

Experiment with different kinds of paint until you find what works best for you.

Stenciling

Stenciling is the process of creating a design by applying paint through open areas on a stencil. The open areas are the positive, printed shapes of the stencil's design. It is an easy and versatile embellishment technique that can add detail or harmony, or it can completely transform your vintage fabric. Create your design using purchased stencils, or make your own.

MATERIALS
+ *Acrylic fabric paint*
+ *Stencil*
+ *Stencil brushes or small cosmetic sponge*
+ *Small bowl of water*
+ *Plastic lids or paper plates for use as a palette*
+ *Plastic spoons for mixing paint*
+ *Paper towels*

Add stenciling to a vintage textile to cover a stain, add color, or just to make a piece your own.

1. Wash and prepare the vintage fabric. Place it right side up on a clean, protected surface.

MAKE YOUR OWN STENCILS

Take inspiration from a vintage piece and cut your own stencil. Find a motif—from embroidery or your fabric—that is simple in design and completely enclosed. The image must be a shape with distinct outlines.

MATERIALS

✦ *Clear acetate sheets (0.005 mm)*
✦ *Transparent tape*
✦ *Cutting mat*
✦ *Craft knife*

1. Place the part of the vintage textile you like on a copy machine. Play with enlarging or reducing the

STEP 2

image until you get the size you want. Outline the photocopied image with a sharp marker.

2. Tape a piece of the acetate on top of the photocopied image. Trace the image onto the acetate with the marker.

STEP 3

3. Place the acetate on the cutting mat. Using the craft knife, cut out the image, cutting the smallest details first. If you accidentally cut into an area, repair it by covering both sides of the acetate with transparent tape and recut.

2. Rinse the brush or sponge in water, then pat out as much water as possible with a paper towel; it should be barely damp.

3. Pour a small amount of paint onto a paper plate. Lightly dip the brush or sponge into the paint, and dab off the excess onto a paper towel. You need a very small amount of paint; otherwise, it will seep underneath the stencil edge (see the photo at right).

4. Holding the edges of the stencil firmly against the fabric, pat the paint into the open areas of the stencil, starting at the center and working out (see the photo on p. 76). Move the stencil around the fabric as you continue the design. Apply as many thin coats of paint

Use a very small amount of paint to prevent seepage under the stencil.

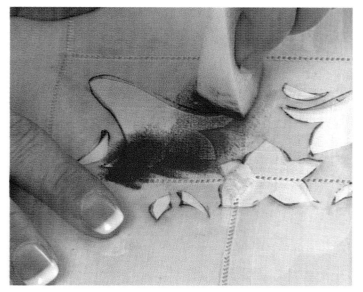

Apply thin coats of paint; thick layers will make the fabric stiff.

If the color and design of the vintage textile are faded and muted, keep the fabric paint in a similar tone and intensity.

as needed, but bear in mind that less is better because thick layers of paint can make the fabric stiff.

5. When finished, allow the paint to dry for 24 hours. Heat-set the cured paint with a dry iron and a press cloth, using the hottest heat setting your fabric will tolerate. Heat-setting will allow you to wash or dry-clean the vintage fabric.

6. Clean stencils by running them under warm water for a few minutes and gently rubbing off the paint. Pat the stencils dry and store in a protective envelope. Wash the stencil brush or sponge in soap and water and allow to air-dry.

If you want to stencil on a dark fabric or want to achieve a more vibrant color, do it in two stages. First apply white paint to the stencil and when it's dry, apply the desired color. To mix colors, layer the paint while it's still wet. To achieve depth, apply the stencil design to the area, then lift the stencil and offset it

slightly. Apply a slightly watered down version of the paint you just used, and you'll get a shadow effect.

Stamping

Stamping is another way to paint a design on the surface of a vintage fabric. Stamps designed specifically for applying paint to fabric have less detail and are cut deeper than stamps designed for paper, making them suitable for applying paint to the textural surface of fabric. Find a stamp that relates to your vintage textile in some way—for example, a flower stamp might pair nicely with a flowered damask pattern on a tablecloth.

Experiment with scraps of fabric, paints, and stencils until you get the look you want. Have fun! If you make a mistake, add an appliqué or beads and call it a "design feature."

TRY THIS

◆ Carry out the theme of the vintage fabric with stamping and stenciling. For example, if you have an embroidered towel with a dog motif that you are using for a child's dress, incorporate a dog bone stamp or stencil into the design.

◆ Use paint to cover an unsuccessful repair on the vintage textile. If it was a really bad repair, appliqué a scrap of the vintage fabric over it and stamp or stencil the area.

◆ Stencil or stamp the lining of a vintage garment, or the back of a pillow or duvet cover. Think about a kimono-style jacket with Japanese stamping on the lining.

MATERIALS

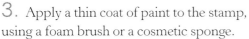

- *Acrylic fabric paint*
- *Stamps designed for use on fabric*
- *Foam brushes or small cosmetic sponges*
- *Plastic lids or paper plates to use as a palette*
- *Small bowl of water*
- *Plastic spoons for mixing paint*
- *Paper towels*

Hold the fabric flat as you lift the stamp to prevent smudging.

1. Wash and prepare the vintage fabric and place it right side up on a clean, protected surface.

2. Pour small amounts of paint onto a lid and mix to get desired colors.

3. Apply a thin coat of paint to the stamp, using a foam brush or a cosmetic sponge.

4. Press the stamp firmly onto the fabric, then lift slowly, holding the fabric flat. Use the stamp one more time for a lighter image or reapply paint to the stamp (see the top photo at right).

5. Continue this process until the design is complete.

6. Allow the painted fabric to cure for 24 hours. Heat-set the designs with a dry iron and a press cloth, using the hottest heat setting your fabric will tolerate. Heat-setting will allow you to wash or dry-clean the vintage fabric.

The flat texture of the wool jersey fabric in this jacket took the stamped image well.

Part of the fun of dyeing a variety of fabrics is that each takes color a little differently.

When dyeing in the washing machine, use a mesh lingerie bag to protect delicate fabrics, but remember that the lingerie bag will also absorb dye and may bleed color the next time you use it.

Dyeing a Vintage Textile

It was my desire to add color to a white damask tablecloth that initially sent me to the dye section of my local hobby store. Since then, I have used dyes to provide unity to dissimilar vintage textiles, to accentuate the weave of a fabric, or to change the color of patterned fabrics, tablecloths, quilt tops, and handkerchiefs. Dyes can be used to change the color of just about any vintage textile, as long as its fiber content is compatible with the dye.

There are many good books available that describe dyeing in great detail, but there are simple ways to achieve a color change in your vintage textile. I have tried a few that I will share with you.

Dyeing in the Washing Machine

The easiest way to dye fabric is with a commercial dye such as RIT, hot water, and your washing machine. This technique will not give you as much control or consistency as other methods and the colors may not be as perma-

nent, so approach this endeavor with flexibility. A vintage textile can be dyed before you cut and sew it, or after construction if your goal is to unify a project with color. This method of dyeing works on fabrics that tolerate hot-water washing, including cotton, rayon, nylon, ramie, linen, silk, wool (which will felt in the process), and acetate.

Here are some tips for dyeing fabrics:

✦ Pretreat the vintage textile to remove stains, because the dye may make them more noticeable.

✦ Prewash fabrics to remove sizing, additives, or any other impurities.

✦ Place delicate textiles in a mesh bag.

✦ Wash most fabrics with a laundry detergent or a scouring agent from a dye supplier, such as Synthrapol (see Resources on p. 133).

✦ Prewash silk, which is a more delicate fiber, using a gentle soap. Set the washing machine on the delicate cycle, and remove the silk fabric before the spin cycle to avoid wrinkles.

✦ Don't dry the textiles; they must be wet for dyeing.

Follow these instructions when dyeing vintage fabrics:

1. Prepare the dye solution according to the manufacturer's recommendations. White or light-colored textiles will dye close to the dye color selected, but if you are starting with bright or dark colors, or if you want to attain a dark color, double the dye quantity.

2. Fill the washing machine with enough hot water for the fabric to move freely. Add the dye solution, and set the machine to agitate five minutes to allow the dye solution to dissipate.

3. Add the wet vintage textile to the dye bath. Set the machine for the longest wash cycle, then check the color. The fabric should be in the dye bath for at least 30 minutes, longer if desired. The color will lighten when the fabric dries.

4. When the desired shade is achieved, rinse in cold water until the water runs clear.

5. Dry the textile in the method that is least destructive to the fabric fibers. If you decide to put the textile in the dryer, use low heat and

Pick out a variety of vintage textiles to dye: quilt blocks, embroidered pieces, lace, handkerchiefs, crocheted pieces, and even buttons.

do not introduce more chemicals by adding fabric softener sheets.

6. Wipe spills with chlorine bleach, and run a complete wash cycle through the washing machine with hot water, detergent, and a cup of bleach before using the machine for regular washing.

Tub Dyeing

Another way to dye a vintage textile is with fiber-reactive dyes. While this method tends to be a little more complicated, the results are reliable and fade resistant. The Procion MX Series is a dye powder that can be used in both cold and hot water. It works well on cotton, linen, rayon, and other cellulose fibers. Basic instructions follow for using this dye; consult the manufacturer's instructions for further guidance (see Resources on p. 133).

MATERIALS
+ *Kitchen scale*
+ *Procion MX Series dye powder (available through dye-supply companies)*
+ *Table salt*
+ *Soda ash*
+ *Large pot made of enamel, stainless steel, or plastic*

1. Weigh the dry fabric. For medium color, you'll need approximately ½ oz. dye for each 1 lb. of dry fabric, decreasing the amount of dye for lighter shades; 1 lb. salt, increasing to 1½ lb. if dyeing navy or black; and ¼ cup soda ash.

I used commercial dye to color a white tablecloth and multicolored silk fabric. Dyeing them together produced fabric for an ensemble.

+ Add laces, trims, cording (and just about anything else that will take dye) with the fabric to be dyed. Sometimes even buttons will take the dye.

+ Don't be afraid to dye patterned and pieced textiles such as quilt tops, curtains, and tablecloths. You never know exactly how they will turn out, but this is half the fun.

+ Make a throw for a sofa from large squares of fabric cut from discarded wool suits. Before piecing the squares together, unify them by dyeing. Add a backing fabric from something unexpected like silk, and use vintage ties for piping around the edges.

Whatever dye method you choose, take precautions and follow the manufacturer's instructions. Wear rubber gloves to protect your skin, and avoid inhaling dye powders when using them. Do not reuse any of the dyeing materials for food preparation, and clean your washing machine thoroughly before adding a regular load.

2. Fill the pot with hot water (105°F); if the fabric is delicate, use cold water. The pot should be made of nonreactive material such as enamel, stainless steel, or durable plastic; do not use an iron, copper, or aluminum pot.

3. Add salt to the pot.

4. Using rubber gloves, make a paste of the dye powder with a small amount of water in a disposable cup, stirring with a plastic spoon. When all the powder has dissolved, thin it with ½ cup water and pour it into the bath; stir.

5. Wet the fabric and put it into the dye bath, stirring constantly for 15 minutes.

6. Remove the fabric and add the soda ash, stirring until it dissolves. Return the fabric to the dye bath.

7. Let the fabric sit in the dye bath, stirring occasionally, 20 to 30 minutes for lighter shades, up to an hour for darker.

8. Remove the fabric from the dye bath and rinse until the water runs clear.

9. Wash the fabric, using the appropriate method. Heat-setting is not required.

BUTTONS AND BUTTONHOLES

With a little imagination and the skills you have, ordinary details like buttons and buttonholes can become design features. Take the techniques you regularly apply in sewing and tweak them using vintage fabric, buttons, and bits and pieces.

Vintage Buttons

Pairing vintage buttons with vintage textiles is a natural combination. And whether you are using old or new fabric, adding vintage buttons to something you have purchased or made gives it a personal touch.

Consider how the button affects the design, but choose what you like, and don't

Use a special vintage button as a purely decorative element. On this wool jersey top, the button is sewn on top of a hook-and-eye closure.

worry if the era or style of the button is different from that of your fabric. If you do not have the exact size and number of buttons the pattern calls for, adjust for size, eliminate a buttonhole, and reposition the others. Try grouping smaller buttons or using just one large vintage button. The buttons don't have to match exactly as long as there is some unifying element: color, size, texture, style, or material.

Covered Buttons

Covered buttons are one way to spruce up a garment or home-decor project such as a pillow or slipcover. Purchase one of the many button-covering kits on the market, and use your vintage fabric and a little imagination to make covered buttons.

Cover buttons with fabric from different areas on an embroidered hand towel for a matching set, each slightly different (see the photo below). Cut the covering for large buttons from a colorful tablecloth or curtains for a stylized look. Take a piece of fabric you have stenciled or stamped, and use it to cover a button. Use pieces of cutwork with contrasting lining, or cover the button with delicately lined vintage lace. The silks in vintage ties make nicely patterned covered buttons, and wool suiting creates a lovely textured button.

If the vintage button you like is too small or needs a little interest, try stacking it on top of another and stitching both of them down.

It can be difficult to find matching vintage buttons for a blouse or jacket. Do the obvious: use mismatched buttons. It will make the garment more interesting.

Add beauty with little effort or expense by covering buttons with bits of vintage fabrics and adding them to clothing and home-decor projects.

Sometimes the garment or project you're working on needs a little pizzazz. Extend some of the techniques you have already used on your vintage garments to the buttons. For example, take a piece of fabric you have stenciled or stamped, and use it to cover a button.

Stacked Buttons

If the vintage button you like is too small or doesn't seem to have enough impact for the design, try stacking the buttons. First, put the larger button, not a shank, against the fabric; it should be a flat button and have two or four holes. Sew it on as you normally would, but as you come back up through the holes of the button for the second or third time, go through the holes or shank of the second button. Continue until the stack of buttons is secure (see the top photo on p. 81).

If you want to use a shank button for the bottom button, glue the top button to it.

TRY THIS

Position a buttonhole so the button becomes part of the design.

✦ Position a buttonhole so the button will complete the design.

✦ Make an inseam buttonhole, and allow the button to slip between the seams. If your pattern does not already have this feature, add a new seam, leaving openings large enough for the buttons to pass through. Inseam buttonholes make an attractive opening for very large or very small buttons, or where the placement of a buttonhole would be distracting.

✦ Add an appliqué of vintage fabric found elsewhere in the garment or home-decor project over the buttonhole area before putting in the buttonhole to unify the design.

Inseam buttonholes are a good choice for very small or large buttons, or where the buttonhole itself would detract from the button or fabric.

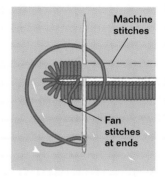

Machine stitches

Fan stitches at ends

✦ Hand-stitch a buttonhole with embroidery floss or cotton or silk buttonhole twist thread to match the rest of a design. To do this, mark the placement line on the right side of the fabric and machine-stitch a rectangle around it, ⅛ in. from the placement line. Cut along the placement line and finish by hand, using small blanket stitches. Fan out the stitches along each end to accommodate for the rectangular shape. For added strength, bar-tack across the ends of the rectangle.

Bead-embellished buttons are easy to do; add as many or few beads as you like.

Beaded Buttons

Simple bead-embellished buttons are easy, even for the bead-challenged. Once the button has been secured with two or three passes of thread, add three or four small beads or one large bead on the front and return the needle to the wrong side of the fabric. Continue adding more beads until you get the design you want, however simple or complex (see the photo above).

Buttonholes and Button Loops

Buttonholes can serve as a design element as well as provide an opening for a button or closure. A cleverly positioned buttonhole can emphasize the beauty of a vintage piece.

Alternatively, button loops are a wise substitute to buttonholes in fragile vintage fabric. They can be a design feature or decorative element as well, especially if the buttons are large or bulky. A button loop can be a sandwiched in the seam between the facing and fabric, for example, at the center front edge of a blouse or vest. Or a button loop and attached cording can be hand-tacked to the right side of the garment to catch the buttons in a series of creatively placed loops, twists, and knots (see the photo at right).

Button loops can be made from purchased cording, but making your own from vintage fabric is much more interesting. Try making an ample length of tubing and playing with its placement. Use tubing as a unifying element between your fabrics, or utilize the loops to emphasize a special vintage button. The button loops can be self-filled tubing, flat tubing, or corded tubing.

Self-Filled Tubing

If you've ever struggled with turning a tube, try this method used by Linda Lee, owner of The Sewing Workshop:

1. To make a self-filled tube, cut a bias strip of fabric four times the width desired for the finished tubing and a piece of pearl cotton 4 in. longer than the desired length.

2. Tie a large knot at one end of the pearl cotton and lay it down the center of the right side of the bias strip, with the knotted end extending out the top. Fold the bias strip in half lengthwise, enclosing the pearl cotton.

3. At the end of the strip with the knot, backstitch across the pearl cotton, then pivot and taper the stitching line out to the center of the strip; sew along the length of the strip (see the top illustration on p. 84).

If you have a couple of really great buttons you'd like to use with different outfits, glue a large snap to the wrong side of each button and sew the other side of the snap to the garment. Now the buttons are interchangeable and can also be removed for laundering.

The button I wanted to use for this vest would have required a very large buttonhole. Instead, I stitched a covered cord to the surface of the vest neckline, catching the end of the cord between the vest front and lining to form a button loop.

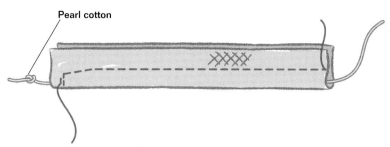

Self-Filled Tubing

Pearl cotton

3. Once the flat tube has been turned, press it flat with the seam positioned in the center, not along a fold.

Flat Tubing as a Button Loop

Flat tubing can be sandwiched in a seam to create a button loop. Use this method to fold the tube:

1. Hold the end of a 3-in. to 4-in. length of tubing in one hand. With the other hand make a fold halfway from the end, bringing the opposite end of the tube down at a right angle. Finger-press the diagonal fold you have created.

2. Now fold the other end of the tube down, creating a sharp point at the top.

3. Stitch across the point (see the illustration below).

4. Sandwich this flat button loop in a seam. The size of the button loop will be determined by how much loop extends from the seam, so make a sample to test with your button.

4. Trim the seam allowance in the area of the backstitching. To turn the tube right side out, pull gently on the loose end of the pearl cotton, easing the knotted end into the tube. Continue to pull the tube through itself until you have a long length of self-filled tubing. Cut off the pearl cotton "tail" close to the seam (see the photo below).

Pull on the knotted end of the cord, pulling the cord through itself to the right side.

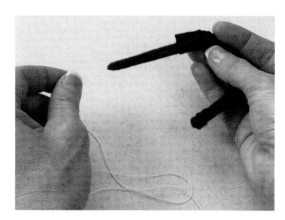

Flat Tubing

Flat tubing is basically a wider form of self-filled tubing, with the filling (the seam allowance) trimmed away:

1. Cut a bias strip of fabric the desired length and twice the width (I prefer at least a 2-in. width of fabric or wider if the fabric is thick) plus seam allowance, and proceed as for self-filled tubing.

2. Before turning the tube, trim the seam allowance to a scant ¼ in.

Making a Button Loop

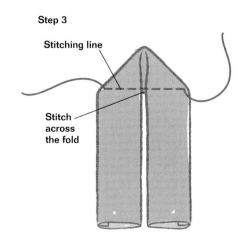

Step 3

Stitching line

Stitch across the fold

Corded Tubing

This technique, which makes classic spaghetti straps, is a little tricky, but once you get the hang of it, you'll find numerous uses for it.

1. Cut a bias strip of fabric the desired length and at least 1 in. wider than the cord circumference. Cut a length of cord twice the length of the bias strip. For cord, purchase filler cord in the desired width, available from crafts and fabric stores, or use rattail, nylon drapery cord, or the cord of your choice.

2. Place the bias strip right side up. Find the midpoint of the cord, and align it at one end of the bias strip, then lay the cord along the center of the strip. Fold the strip in half lengthwise, encasing the cord.

3. Using the zipper foot, stitch across the end of the bias strip, through the midpoint of the cord, then pivot and sew along the length of strip next to the cord (see the illustration below). Do not catch the cord as you stitch along the strip.

4. Trim the seam allowance to ¼ in.

5. To turn the tube right side out, use your fingers to ease the fabric at the stitched end of the bias tube over the exposed cord. Then pull on the loose end of the cord and continue to ease the bias over itself. When the tube is turned, cut off the extending cord close to the seam.

6. If you want to finish the open end of the covered cord, slide the bias away from the cord end and cut off about ½ in. of cord. Tuck in the bias end and stitch closed.

Whatever your sewing skills and techniques, including the ones I have discussed, use them in creative ways to enhance your vintage tex-

tile. Sometimes just a small detail like a covered button gives your design individuality. You'll see how easy some of these techniques really are.

TRY THIS

+ Use vintage tie silk to cover a cord. Wind the length of cord down the front edge of a blouse or jacket, and leave a loop to accommodate a large vintage button.

+ Piece together kimono pieces to cover a cord. Sew cording into the seam of a purse flap for a button closure, or use it for the purse handle.

+ Expand the idea of cording as a button loop, and consider cording as a trim or surface embellishment. Let the cord meander across the vintage fabric in a pleasing design and tack it down.

+ Cover narrow cording with vintage fabric, and use it to attach a large-holed button. Tack down the cord in the middle, run each end of the cord through the holes of the button, and tie a knot on the button top.

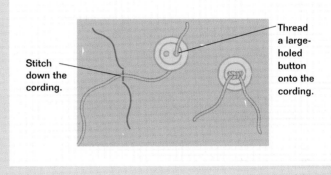

Stitch down the cording.

Thread a large-holed button onto the cording.

Corded Tubing

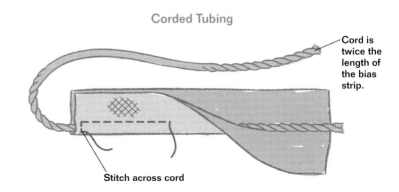

Cord is twice the length of the bias strip.

Stitch across cord

A PERFECT PURSE

If you're hesitant to try some of the techniques we've discussed, start small. Using a special vintage textile, make a purse or bag for yourself or as a gift. A fragile piece can be made into a special-occasion bag, or you can sew a sturdy vintage piece to a background fabric to create a bag for everyday use. Combine fabrics and embellish them with laces, trims, and beading. You can purchase a commercial pattern, or make a rectangular or square purse in a size that works for you. In the following example, a vintage silk scarf was sewn to the purse front before construction.

Modify the following instructions to work with your vintage textile, and adjust the size to create a simple bag.

This construction method may be unfamiliar to you, but when you slip your hand inside the bag between the vintage fabric layers and turn it right side out, it really does work. This is the neatest, foolproof way I've found to make a lined pouch.

This vintage purse holds nostalgia as well as necessities. Who would know it was made from a silk scarf?

MATERIALS

- Vintage textile: tapestry, needlepoint, silk scarf, embroidered piece, quilt top, etc., cut to 9 in. by 11½ in.
- Fabric for purse front and back, each 8½ in. by 11 in.
- Fabric for lining front and back, each 8½ in. by 11 in.
- ½ yd. fabric to cover purse handle and for bias binding
- Knit fabric for button loop, 1 in. by 5 in., cut crosswise
- ½ in. diameter cording, 42 in. long
- Quilt batting or cotton flannel for front and back interlining, each 8½ in. by 11 in.
- 1 large button

1. For binding the purse top edge, cut a bias strip of fabric 1¾ in. by 17 in. Set aside.

2. For the purse handle, cut the cord 42 in. To cover the cord, cut a bias strip of fabric 2½ in. by 42 in.

3. Press the edges of the vintage piece under ¼ in., and topstitch to the purse top.

4. Stack the fabrics as follows:

- purse front and back, right sides together
- one layer of interlining
- front and back lining pieces, right sides together
- last layer of interlining

Make your purse as individual as you are by decorating it with trim or lining the inside with a silky tablecloth.

STEP 11 Baste the ends of the handle over each side seam on the right side of the purse.

STEP 12 Flip the handles up at the side seams over the completed bias edging and topstitch in place.

5. Turn the stacked fabrics over so the purse fabric is on top. Pin all layers together.

6. Using a ½-in. seam allowance and leaving one short end open, sew the layers together along the edges. Finish the seam allowance edge if desired.

7. Slip your hand between the purse front and back layers, turning the bag right side out. Baste the lining, interlining, and purse fabric together at the top edge of the purse.

8. To make the button loop, refer to p. 83 for making self-filled tubing.

9. Fold the button loop in half. Baste it to the right side of the purse back at the center top edge, aligning the ends of the loop with the edge of the bag.

10. To make the purse handle, refer to p. 85 for making corded tubing.

11. Place the ends of the purse handle over the purse side seams, right sides together. Baste in place.

12. Sew the bias edging to the purse top, following the instructions for binding an edge on pp. 41–43. Flip the handles up at the side seams over the completed bias edging and topstitch in place (see the bottom left photo above).

Here are some more ideas for making beautiful handbags:

+ If you find a damaged or incomplete vintage needlepoint piece, cut away the unusable portions and use the rest for a purse front. Refer to pp. 66–67 for guidelines for finishing the needlepoint

Kimono pieces were randomly pieced, quilted, and beaded for this purse. I lined it with old ties and used vintage beads for the fringe and an old button for the closure.

edges, and if desired, blocking the needlepoint. Construct the purse in the manner described above, eliminating the interlining for the purse front. Use a decorative trim for the purse handle, line the purse with a vintage tablecloth, and add a small pocket. Add purchased beaded fringe, or refer to beading books to make your own. (See Resources on p.133.)

+ Create a purse from a recycled sweater. If the knitted fabric is likely to lose its shape, first sew it to a backing fabric.

CHAPTER FIVE

CREATIVE CLOTHING FOR CHILDREN

Whether you are creating an heirloom christening gown or small-fry overalls, vintage fabrics will make the garment special. Children are easy to fit, and if they're younger than eight years old, they're not usually particular about what's "in." Their main desire is for comfortable clothing that is fun to wear. Find a soft, colorful tablecloth, cozy, patterned sweater, or a coat that is on its way to The Salvation Army, and get inspired.

Take a look at vintage textiles in a new light. True, many are white and delicate, but many more are colorful, sturdy, and waiting to be used creatively. Don't be concerned that your child may stain or ruin them—where are they now? Pull them out of that box or off that closet shelf and take advantage of their soft patina to create a kid-friendly garment.

THE "GROWTH FACTOR"

Consider adding extra fabric to children's clothing, since they seem to outgrow everything at an astonishing rate. Ask yourself this question when sewing anything for children: How can the style, design, and construction be adapted to utilize the most wear time? In the case of working in vintage fabrics, the answer to this question is a must.

If you are making an heirloom garment the child will wear only a few times, don't worry about designing it to grow. For all other garments, however, you want your time and

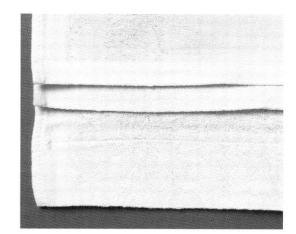

Stitch the tucks in place and press toward the hem.

effort to go toward producing a favorite that will fit them as long as possible.

Pattern and Style Selection for Children

Select a pattern design that is loose fitting, generously sized, and has a length that can be adjusted. If you are making a dress for your daughter or granddaughter, avoid a fitted pattern and make it on the long side, with a deep hem. You also can add a few tucks above the hem and remove them as your child grows. Avoid elastic at the wrist and ankles, which might bind as a child grows, and avoid designs that fit too closely to the neck. Use roll-back cuffs on jackets and coats, which can be rolled down as his or her arms lengthen. Add to the wear time of children's pants and shirts by sewing a fold-up knit cuff to the bottom of pant legs or long sleeves and unfold it as the child grows.

Tucks

To create tucks along the hem of a child's dress:

1. Decide the depth of the tucks (when sewn and pressed) and the distance between the tucks. In this example, each tuck is ½ in. deep with 1 in.

Add tucks to the bottom of a child's dress and remove them for added length as she grows.

between tucks. The lower edge of the bottom tuck is 2 in. above the lower edge of the dress, which has a 1¼-in. hem. So the overall cut length of the skirt in this example is the desired length plus 1 in. for each tuck plus 1¾ in. for the hem, plus the waistline seam allowance.

2. To form the skirt hem, press the raw edge of the hem allowance up ¼ in., then fold up 1½ in., press, and stitch. With the right side of the skirt up, use a chalk marker and a ruler to mark a line parallel to and 2½ in. above the skirt hemline. Mark another line 1 in. above this line. Mark a third and fourth line, spacing them at 1-in. intervals.

3. With wrong sides together, match up the two lower lines and stitch together. Match the two upper lines and stitch together. Press the tucks down toward the hem.

Knit Cuffs

This technique provides an easy way lengthen pants or sleeves. The method for pants is explained here; it's easy to adapt for sleeves:

1. To determine the size of the knit ribbing, measure the circumference of your child's ankle and add 2 in. (more or less according to your child's size) to allow for seam allowance

Attach vintage napkins to baby T-shirts to make a special dress. Take advantage of a tablecloth's border print to make a child's jumper.

and ease. Cut a crosswise piece of knit ribbing this long and 12 in. deep (more or less).

2. Fold the ribbing in half, right side in, aligning the 12-in. edges. Sew into a tube, using a ¼-in. seam allowance. Turn right side

If your child finds the armholes of a sleeve scratchy, encase the seam allowances in cotton or polyester bias binding or washable satin ribbon.

STEP 2 **Make a long tube and fold it in half for the cuff.**

STEP 3 **Be sure to stretch the cuff as you sew it to the pant leg so the ankle opening is big enough for a child's foot.**

out. Fold, wrong sides together and raw edges even, to make a doubled tube 6 in. deep.

3. Sew two rows of basting stitches along the bottom edge of each leg of the pants. With right sides together and matching the seam of the ribbing to the inside pant-leg seam, gather the pant leg to fit the knit ribbing. Stretch the ribbing moderately as you pin it to the pant leg—remember, your child's foot has to go through it. With cuff side up, stitch in place, using a narrow zigzag stitch of medium length and a ⅜-in. seam allowance.

4. Roll the knit cuff up to the desired length. As the child grows, the tube can be unrolled to add length.

If you add a knit cuff to the bottom of your child's pants, the cuff can be turned down as she grows.

Cut the cuffs off worn socks and attach them to pant legs or sleeves.

MAKE IT KID-FRIENDLY

Sewing for a child can bring the kid out in you. Kid-friendly clothes are comfortable, easy, fun for your child to wear, and are designed to promote independence. The garments you sew should be the two or three things your child wants to wear over and over. You want your time and effort to go toward producing one of these favorites.

Fabric Choices

Good-quality materials, whether old or new, will last as your child grows. Choose fabrics that can withstand the wear and tear of children, launder well, require minimal, if any, ironing, and pick fabrics that have a soft, appealing texture. Damaged areas of vintage fabrics, including holes and stains, are workable as long as the areas aren't too big and the rest of the fabric is sturdy. Encourage your child to participate in designing the garment and choosing the fabric, buttons, and trims.

The Comfort Zone

We all know a child who can't stand anything that is remotely scratchy against his skin. He brings you the scissors with each new shirt and says, "Cut off the tag." He rolls down the waistband of elastic pants and shorts because he doesn't like it against his skin. He can't stand to wear a monogrammed shirt, and he'll wear only one style of socks.

I have no solution for the socks other than turning them wrong side out so the toe seam is not against the skin. And as for the monogrammed shirt, if it's the stabilizer on the back of the stitching that's the problem, cut it off close to the stitching. If it is still uncomfortable for your child, fuse a square of soft cotton or washable satin over the back of the monogram.

Soft Elastic Waistband

To construct a soft elastic waistband for a pair of pants or shorts you are making, omit the self-casing waistband and replace it with a sewn-on casing made of soft cotton or poly-

ester. Then make sure the elastic is not too tight in combination with the softer waistband; this should make the pants more comfortable for your child.

1. Follow the pattern directions for cutting out and constructing the pants or shorts until you are ready to fold over the waistband to form a casing for the elastic.

2. Cut off the waistband casing, leaving ⅜ in. for a seam allowance. Cut a piece of soft fabric (cotton, polyester, etc.) equal in length but ⅜ in. deeper than the waistband casing just removed.

My daughter loved this dress. As she grew, she rolled the sleeve cuffs down and wore it as a shirt with pants underneath.

Let your children participate in designing garments, picking the fabrics and trims. The combinations may not be your first choice, but they will love them.

3. With right sides in, sew the ends of the new waistband together to form a ring. With the right sides together and the seams aligned at the center back, pin and then sew the waistband to the pants or shorts. Trim the seam allowances and press toward the waistband. Continue construction according to the pattern instructions.

Independence

Depending on the age of the child, independence may be a big issue. He may have strong opinions about dressing himself and about what he wants to wear. Design clothing that allows your child the independence he wants. Try the suggestions that follow.

To promote children's independence with dressing, sew a piece of satin ribbon into the back neckline or waistband to identify the garment back. Use a fabric-marking pen to add the child's name or initials. To designate that a set goes together, use the same colored ribbon for the top and bottom.

CREATIVE USES FOR VINTAGE TEXTILES

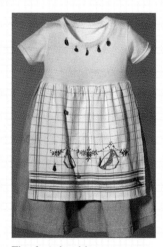

The fruit baubles were my daughter's idea. She wanted them sewn at the neckline to be her necklace.

✦ Embroidered tea towels: Combine with other fabrics to use as an apron on a little girl's dress or as a collar. Or appliqué them to the surface of a vest, jacket or dress.

✦ Cotton, rayon, and linen tablecloths: Use to make dresses, jackets, blouses, shirts, and more. Use the tablecloth by itself or combine it with other vintage tablecloths, tea towels, quilts, etc.

✦ Wool, cotton, and acrylic blankets, and quilts: Use to make jackets or vests, or use inside a jacket for a cozy lining.

✦ Sweaters and mittens: Recycle into pockets, purses, vests, hats, and jackets.

✦ Wool suits: Cut a vest or jacket from the worn suit, then dye it and embellish it with laces, buttons, and trims.

Combine the wool suiting with old sweaters to make a jacket.

✦ Wedding gowns: Create an heirloom christening gown, or a special-occasion dress for a little girl. Dye the wedding-gown fabric and combine with a T-shirt for a simple dress.

✦ Recycled furs: Make a fur muff, teddy bear, vest, or purse.

✦ Lace, buttons, trims, and beads: Kids love embellishments—the wackier the better. Use big, bright, vintage buttons if you can find them; put lace around a plain pocket; put dangling baubles around a neckline; use vintage pieces for closures and embellishments.

- When garments call for buttons, make the buttons large and the buttonholes somewhat loose. Large buttons are easier for little fingers to grasp, and loose buttonholes ensure the child won't have to struggle to get the button through the hole. Use odd, old buttons saved from flea-market treasures, and mix them for a fun look. Make knit button loops instead of button holes for easy maneuvering.

- If a garment calls for a zipper, consider using a large-tooth variety and tying a ribbon or bauble onto the pull tab to make it easier to manipulate. Or replace the zipper with hook-and-loop fasteners.

- When possible, put buttons and zippers in the front of the garment so they can be reached.

- Choose pants styles with elasticized waists. They are easier to pull up and down.

- Avoid belts. They come undone, are left undone, or get lost.

- If you are sewing for a little girl, a jumper may be more practical than a dress. Your child can choose whether to wear it with a long- or short-sleeve shirt or no shirt at all.

- Add pockets. They hold many important treasures. Put them on dresses, vests, pants, and skirts—old bandannas, handkerchiefs, and cocktail napkins are clever choices. If you are making a coat for a child, add large inside pockets to hold mittens. To decrease bulk, make these pockets out of lining or another lightweight fabric. Put a hook-and-loop closure across the pocket top; your

Preshrink rayon lining fabric and use it to make a comfortable waistband.

If you add pockets to your child's clothing be sure to remove the treasures they collect before laundering!

child will be less likely to lose his mittens with a closed inside pocket. The challenge, of course, is to get him to put them in there!

- Encourage your children to use their own outgrown or worn "vintage" clothing, like sweaters and socks, in clothing designs for themselves. Let them participate by picking out fabrics, buttons, trims, and embellishments and helping with the arrangement.

- Make outfits that are interchangeable—tops that go with multiple bottoms and vice versa.

- Dress patterns for little girls often include belt straps that tie in the back, which, unfortunately, tend to come untied and land in the toilet. Eliminate the tie straps altogether and replace with a fabric-covered elasticized band—sewn in or attached with suspender clips.

Pretty Elasticized Band

Gather in the back of a loose dress with a fabric-covered elasticized band. These are great for using up small bits of wonderful old fabric and—no more untied ties! (see the photo below).

If a dress is a little big or has too much fullness, make a suspender clip to cinch it in.

1. Cut a 4-in. length of ¾-in.- to 1-in.-wide elastic. Cut a piece of fabric 10 in. long and 3 in. wide.

2. Fold the fabric in half lengthwise, right sides together. Using a ¼-in. seam allowance, sew along the long edge. Trim the seam allowance and turn the tube right side out. Press so the seam lies along the middle of the tube, not along a folded edge.

3. Attach a safety pin or bodkin to the elastic; thread it part way through the tube. Pin the loose end of the elastic even with the end of the tube. Continue threading the elastic through the tube, then pin the elastic to the end of the tube. Zigzag across each end of the tube to secure the elastic to the gathered fabric.

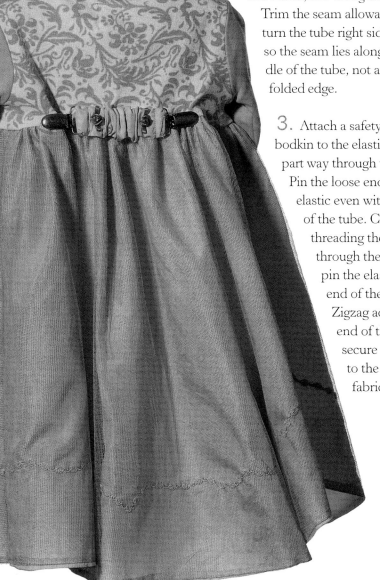

The ends for these elasticized suspender clips are available in crafts stores, or recycle a pair of mitten clips.

The embellishments you add to the suspender clips don't need to be washable, so get creative!

4. If the band is to be sewn to the dress, turn each end under ½ in. and baste. If you are making a removable band, attach suspender clips to each end; slip the ends of the strip through the suspender clips, and stitch in place.

5. Embellish the band with vintage buttons, ribbons, silk flowers, etc., making sure the elastic is still stretchable.

6. Experiment with the placement of the band in the lower back region of the dress.

The band should gather the dress 2 in. or more without making it too tight. Pin in place and topstitch, or secure with the clips.

CREATIVE CLOTHING IDEAS

Let me give you some additional ideas for sewing creative children's clothing using vintage textiles. Your fabrics, patterns, and children are different from mine, so some of these designs are shared as ideas only, while for others they are complete instructions.

T-Shirt Dress with Apron

When my daughters were young, I made them many of these simple, apron-trimmed T-shirt dresses, which are easy to make and wear. As the girls got older, they participated by picking out the fabric, T-shirt, tea towel for the apron, and button, bead, and bauble embellishments. Follow along as I show you how to make a toddler size 3 dress, with a skirt length of 20 in. Adjust the measurements for the size you are making. Before you begin, be sure to launder the materials as you will the dress so after-the-fact shrinkage won't spoil your work.

MATERIALS
◆ *1 size 3 T-shirt*
◆ *Fabric for the skirt (see step 1)*
◆ *1 tea towel*
◆ *Assortment of buttons, baubles, ribbons, laces*

1. The fullness of the skirt is determined by the fabric width. Use two widths if the fabric is 45 in. wide or less and one width if the fabric is 54 in. to 60 in. wide. To determine the length of the skirt, have the child put on the T-shirt. Measure from 2 in. below the armhole to the desired length; add ⅝ in. for the top

The bark cloth, flannel, and cotton velveteen were washed prior to construction, increasing the practicality of this outfit.

seam allowance and whatever hem allowance you wish.

2. Measure the distance from the bottom edge of the T-shirt to 2⅝ in. below the armhole. With an erasable pen or chalk marker, mark a line this distance above the bottom edge across the front and back of the shirt.

You can make this simple dress in less than two hours.

center front and center back. Sew two lines of basting stitches around the top of the skirt, ¼ in. and ½ in. below the raw edge.

5. Mark the center front and center back lower edge of the T-shirt. Gather the skirt to fit the T-shirt, and with right sides together and cut edges aligned, pin them together, matching center fronts, center backs, and side seams (see the top right photo on the facing page).

6. Adding the tea towel apron to the skirt front is not an exact science. In this example I wanted the apron to be about 5 in. shorter than the skirt so I cut the tea towel to be 15⅜ in. long. Cut yours as you wish, bearing in mind the position of any decorative pattern. Sew two lines of gathering stitches along the top (the cut) edge of the tea towel and gather it in so that it covers most of the front of the skirt. Adjust the gathers or the length until the effect looks good to you.

7. Remove the pins holding the skirt front to the T-shirt, and insert the tea towel between the skirt and the T-shirt, wrong side of towel to right side of the skirt. Pin the apron to the skirt, then pin the skirt back to the T-shirt (see the bottom left photo on the facing page).

Cut along this line to remove the lower part of the T-shirt (see the top left photo on the facing page).

3. To make the skirt, sew each side seam and finish the seam edges. Press up the hem allowance as planned and topstitch in place.

4. On the top edge of the skirt, mark the points halfway between the side seams for the

8. Starting at a side seam and using a ⅜-in. seam allowance, sew the skirt and apron to the T-shirt. Finish the seam and press toward the T-shirt.

9. Add buttons and embellishments: Sew vintage buttons or covered buttons down the center of the T-shirt, along the T-shirt/skirt seamline, or around the neckline of the T-shirt. If the dress seems wide around the child's torso, draw it in with a suspender clip.

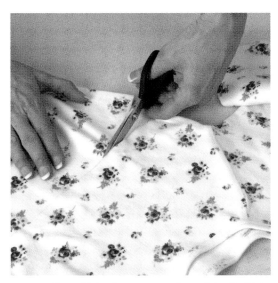

STEP 2 Cut off the bottom portion of the T-shirt.

STEP 5 Gather the top edge of the skirt to fit the T-shirt.

Another way to gather a skirt is to zigzag over a string or pearl cotton thread. Lay the string ½ in. from the cut edge of the top of the skirt and set your machine for the widest zigzag stitch. Zigzag over the string without catching it in the stitching. Pull on the string to gather in the skirt.

STEP 7 Insert the apron between the T-shirt and skirt.

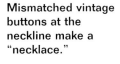

Mismatched vintage buttons at the neckline make a "necklace."

Tablecloth Dress

I used colorful floral tablecloths from the '50s and '60s combined with vintage laces, trims, buttons, and embellishments to make dresses for my daughters when they were young. It seemed no matter what the combinations were, big prints, loud colors, or dancing vegetables, or how many design rules were broken, the dresses always looked great. Find a few colorful tablecloths and give it a try.

In the example at left, I used a pattern that had a full skirt attached to a bodice front and back with cap sleeves. Because of the small size of the tablecloth, I added panels of new fabric to the center of the bodice front and back and used a contrasting fabric for flat piping and the bias band neckline and sleeve finishes.

Vintage buttons add fun accents. I used a button loop and only one button at the neckline for the back closure because my daughter told me "buttons poke." If you look closely at the design of flowers on the skirt, you can see that the pattern is not symmetrical. The small size of the tablecloth and the way the border was printed onto the fabric made it impossible to get the design equal at both sides of the skirt—but I think the resulting asymmetry is interesting.

Vintage tablecloths that have been laundered many times have a soft hand and seem to wrinkle less, making them perfect fabric for a child's dress.

Vintage handkerchiefs were used to make smaller bag pockets on this top.

TRY THIS

The pocket is formed by folding the bag up and topstitching along each side.

+ Add pockets to the dress, sandwiching them between the skirt and T-shirt. For each pocket, cut two pieces of fabric 5 in. by 10 in. With right sides together, sew along the two long sides and one short side using a ⅝-in. seam. Trim the seams, press, and turn the pieces right side out. For each pocket, fold one of the pieces crosswise, aligning the finished end about 3 in. below the unfinished end. Pin the sides together. Use an edge-stitch foot, and top-stitch ⅛ in. from the edge (see the photo at left). Insert the unfinished end of the pocket between the T-shirt and the skirt, making sure the pocket opening will face out when the dress is finished.

+ Add vintage lace to the lower edge of a skirt or to a petticoat under the skirt. Add ribbon roses, buttons, or baubles around the T-shirt neckline.

+ Use a vintage handkerchief, dresser scarf, or the corner of an embroidered tablecloth instead of a tea towel for the apron.

+ If you want to make the tea towel removable (for example, if you want to launder it separately from the dress, or add it to the dress only some of the time), finish the top of the towel. Then add buttonholes near the top edge and place corresponding buttons on the dress bodice.

+ If your child is potty-training, hem the dress above her knees so it won't be so likely to dip into the toilet!

Cozy Coat

I love sewing with vintage linens, but when the weather turns cold, I can't wait to sew with wool. I made the jacket shown on p. 103 for my daughter and used many of the techniques discussed in chapter 4, using wool melton, wool knit jersey, and recycled sweater pieces. I used pink dye on the wool jersey for the collar, covered buttons, and binding for the collar and pockets. I had little control over the technique but was nonetheless pleased with the outcome. I took the sweater apart at the seams, serged the edges to prevent raveling, and machine-washed and dried it to get the fulled, blurred appearance, and texture.

The pattern was for a boxy, thigh-length coat with a Peter Pan collar. For ease of construction and to minimize the bulk and weight

Topstitching the seam allowance open helps keep this bulky fabric flat.

Fix a sagging pocket by stitching it in place with a short run of satin stitches down the center of the top pocket edge.

Itchy necklines and seamlines can be a curse: Cover the offending area with ribbon.

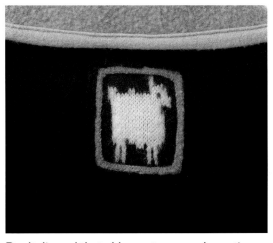

Don't discard that old sweater; recycle portions of it and use it for reverse appliqué.

of the coat, the edges were finished with wool-jersey binding. The steps, below, are guidelines on how I made this particular garment; adjust them to suit your project.

MATERIALS

+ *1½ yd. navy wool melton*
+ *¼ yd. pink wool melton*
+ *¼ yd. pink wool jersey*
+ *¼ yd. navy wool jersey*
+ *Recycled sweater*
+ *Coat jacket pattern*
+ *Button cover kit*

1. I first modified the pattern by removing the ⅝-in. seam allowance along the front opening and neckline, back neckline, collar outer edge, and the hem from the front, back, and sleeve. The pattern pieces were cut out of the melton. Because the collar was attached as a single layer, only one collar piece was cut. Because all the edges were to be bound, I omitted all facings and interfacings. I made a pattern in a shape and size I liked for the pockets—in this case, they went across the lower portion of each jacket front.

2. The technique for making binding and attaching it to the wool jacket is similar to the bias binding description given in chapter 3, with two exceptions. Because the binding fabric is knit, I cut it on the cross-grain instead of the bias, and because the wool fabric is thick, I cut the binding wider to accommodate the turn of the cloth. I cut 2-in. strips of pink wool jersey to bind the pockets and collar, and cut and seamed together 2-in. strips of navy wool jersey to get the needed length for the rest of the jacket.

3. I assembled the jacket, placing the pieces right sides together and using ⅜-in. seam allowances throughout. Each jacket shoulder was sewn, finger-pressed open and top-stitched ½ in. on each side of the seam (see the top left photo on the facing page). The sleeves were sewn to the body of the jacket and the armscye seam allowances on the body of the jacket were trimmed to ¼ in. The sleeve seam allowance was finger-pressed toward the body and topstitched in place, ½ in. from the seam.

4. I marked the pockets on the sweater fabric using a chalk marker. To keep the fabric from unraveling, I stitched a narrow zigzag over each chalk line, then cut out the pockets, just outside the zigzag stitching. Using a ⅜-in. seam allowance, I bound the top edge of each pocket with pink wool jersey. I folded the raw edge of the binding almost to the seam allowance before wrapping the binding over the edges, onto the right side, and topstitched it in place.Once this was done, I basted the pockets

to the jacket fronts, aligning the cut edges on the sides and bottom and turning under the center front edge of each pocket ½ in. Because the pockets were so wide, once each was sewn to the jacket, I used a satin stitch over the binding to hold the center of the top edge in place (see the top right photo on the facing page).

5. I sewed each side seam from the bottom of the body to the bottom of the sleeve, catch-

I was short on fabric for the sleeves. Adding the pink wool inset provided the needed length.

3 in. from the starting place so I could sew the ends of the binding together.

6. Before attaching the collar, I bound its outside edge. To avoid bulk at the neckline, I overlapped the jacket neckline onto the collar. First, I basted the placement line on the collar in contrasting thread, ⅝ in. from the edge. I put the collar wrong side up (the "under collar" side) on my table, and, holding the jacket right side up, aligned the bound edge of the neckline with the basting and pinned it in place. I sewed the jacket to the collar, stitching over the binding topstitching. To avoid an itchy neckline, I sewed a piece of grosgrain ribbon over the collar seam allowance on the inside of the jacket (see the bottom left photo on p. 102).

7. Using the reverse appliqué technique described in chapter 4, a square piece of the sweater fabric was centered in the upper back of the jacket, sewn into place, and the outer wool fabric cut away revealing the appliqué (see the bottom right photo on p. 102).

Wedding Gown to Christening Gown

If you have a wedding gown that has sentimental value yet want to see it used in your daily life, or even one you've found at a garage sale, turn it into a different kind of heirloom that can be worn by many new family members. Look at the wedding gown differently and don't be afraid to cut it up—consider it a source for yards and yards of fabric and lace to make a christening gown. The wedding gown and christening-gown pattern you choose will be different from the one I used, so use the following information as suggestion for how to create your own.

If you have any doubts about your wedding gown being clean, send it to the dry cleaner, hand-wash it, or put it in the washer and dryer, with a few preparatory steps. Remove any detachable sections first, such as the train.

Consider a recycled wedding gown as a source for yards of fabric and lace and make a special christening gown.

ing the pocket edge in the side seam. The seam allowances were finger-pressed open and topstitched ½ in. on each side of the seams. Beginning at a bottom side seam, I pinned the binding to the wrong side of the jacket edge. I sewed the binding on, stitching all the way around the jacket but stopping

TRY THIS

✦ Use Polarfleece instead of wool. Like wool melton, Polarfleece doesn't ravel, so it is a good fabric for reverse appliqué. Or use recycled acrylic mittens for pockets and reverse appliqué pieces.

✦ Don't bother to finish the edges. Because they won't ravel, wool melton and Polarfleece can be finished with a decorative cut edge, using a rotary cutter with a pinked or wavy blade.

✦ Use an old wool blanket that has been softened with repeated washing and line it with a vintage cotton sheet or blanket—or cotton flannel.

✦ If you can find a good piece of bark cloth—textured woven cotton used to make curtains and other upholstery items—use it to make a warm, cozy coat.

1. Lay out the gown on a clean sheet on the floor and check the various layers for stains and damage. If possible, determine the gown's fabric content and see if it can handle the rigors of a washing machine.

2. Cut two 4-in. squares, serge or zigzag the edges, and machine-wash and dry. Use cool or warm water and a delicate wash cycle. Dry one swatch in the dryer on low heat and let the other air-dry. If neither of the swatches survive, hand-wash or dry-clean the gown.

3. If the dress has hook-and-eye closures or hook-and-loop tape, remove them so they do not snag the lace and tulle. If there is loose or ripped tulle or lace, repair it or cut it off so it won't get caught in the machine.

4. Wash the veil in a lingerie bag or by hand and air-dry. Wash the dress and train separately so they don't become tangled. Dry the

The train of this wedding dress was dyed blue and turned wrong side out for the skirt of this T-shirt dress.

dress in the dryer or allow it to dry over a rack. If it gets stiff with air-drying, put it in the dryer with a moist towel on the air-dry setting for 15 to 30 minutes.

After the gown has dried thoroughly, lay it on top of the sheet again. Ask yourself these questions:

+ Have the stains been removed? If not, can you work around them?
+ Have new areas of damage appeared? Can you fix them?
+ Do you like the color? If you think you want to dye it, consider dyeing one of the test swatches first to see how it takes.

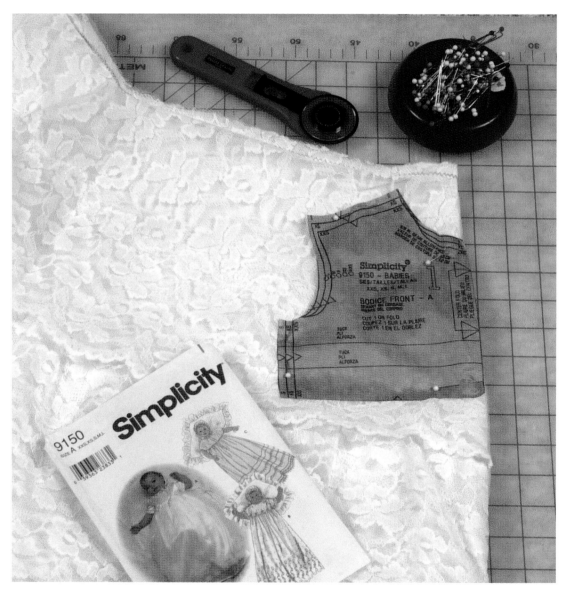

You may have to modify some of the pattern pieces to take advantage of a specific area of lace or other detail on the wedding gown, but fortunately, fitting requirements for a christening gown are minimal.

+ Are there big pieces of fabric and lace that can be used in their entirety? For example, can the taffeta lining of the gown be used for the front and back skirt of the christening gown?

+ What does the reverse side of the fabric look like? And what about the layers of fabric that are sometimes hidden between or underneath the top layers? So much fabric is used to make a wedding gown that you may not appreciate a beautiful piece unless you dig.

Find a christening-gown pattern you like, and look at the line drawings on the back of the envelope; look at the actual pattern pieces as well. Can you imagine how the pattern pieces will be placed on the wedding gown? Are there ways the wedding gown, as constructed, can be used? For example, if there are tiers of gathered lace attached to a background fabric, can you cut a pattern piece from this fabric combination? (See the photo on the facing page.)

When I brought home a wedding gown from a thrift store to make the christening gown shown on p. 104, my family questioned my sanity. True, it was dingy, yellowed, and had an odor, but it also had potential. The dress had tiers of gathered, wide lace attached to a taffeta skirt, and between the lace and taffeta were layers of tulle.

I let the wedding gown air outside for a few days, in hopes the odor would disappear. I repaired areas where the lace had ripped, and removed the train and the hook-and-eye closures that attached the train to the dress. Using the train as my test swatch, I washed it on a gentle cycle in warm water and mild detergent, and dried it on low heat. I was pleasantly surprised to find the color was a creamy white and the lace had softened considerably,

TRY THIS

Recycle other garments into clothing for children:

+ Make a frilly tutu from an old wedding or prom dress.

+ Wash and dry several wool sweaters and make a small coat. Cut a sleeve from one sweater, a front from another sweater, etc.

+ Use old blue jeans and flannel shirt to outfit a little cowboy: make a vest, skirt, or small backpack.

Use a delicately embroidered vintage handkerchief or tablecloth to make a bonnet to go with the christening gown.

so I felt confident washing and drying the entire dress the same way. In preparation for cutting out my pattern, I ripped out the side seams of the dress and laid the skirt front on my cutting mat.

I chose a christening-gown pattern with a bodice, short sleeves, and a long, full skirt. I laid out the pattern pieces for the front and back skirt, which were rectangles, on the wedding dress skirt front, and cut them out. The bodice and sleeves were cut from the wedding dress skirt back, which was a taffeta-over-tulle combination. I flipped this fabric combination over, however, because I wanted the tulle to be on the outside of the bodice and sleeves. The christening gown was constructed according to the pattern directions. Lace from the wedding dress was added to the sleeves, and vintage buttons were used down the back.

TOOTH-FAIRY PILLOW

If you've ever spent anxious minutes in your child's bedroom searching frantically for the tooth that is supposed to be under the pillow, you'll appreciate this project. Make a tooth-fairy pillow large enough to make the stealthy exchange easier and add a pocket to secure the tooth. In this example, you will create an envelope-style case with a dinner napkin—both square and rectangular napkins will work. You can adapt the method easily to suit any vintage textile—just cut to the desired size and serge or zigzag all edges before beginning. Minimal time and sewing skill are required for this project. The beauty is in the napkin. Before beginning, launder and lightly starch the napkin.

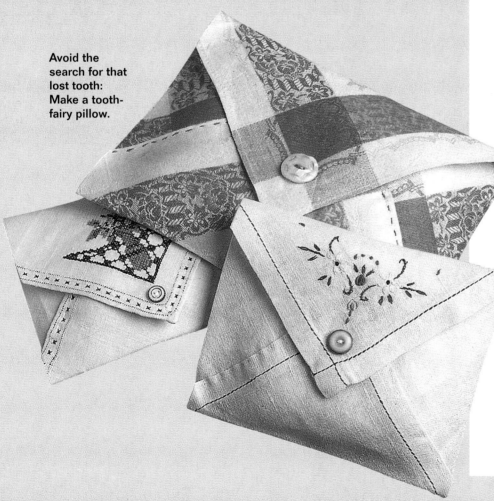

Avoid the search for that lost tooth: Make a tooth-fairy pillow.

MATERIALS

- *1 vintage napkin*
- *1 button*
- *¼ yd. or less white fabric for pillow and pocket*
- *2 in. hook-and-loop tape*
- *Pinking-blade rotary cutter or pinking shears*
- *Batting or stuffing for pillow*

1. If you have trouble understanding the folds for this project, open up the sides of a paper envelope and refer to it as you go along. Lay the napkin wrong side up on your ironing board, oriented on the diagonal. Fold the two side corners toward the middle so they meet. Press in place. Fold the bottom corner up so it overlaps the two sides by approximately ⅝ in. Press and pin in place.

2. Fold the remaining corner toward the center, overlapping it so the point is an inch or two from the bottom edge of the case. Press.

3. Unfold the top corner, which will be the envelope flap. Hand stitch the remaining overlapped edges from the lower left corner to the center point, then to the lower right corner. Make sure you catch only the top two layers of fabric, not the pillow back.

4. Cut a ½-in. square of hook-and-loop tape and sew the loop portion of the tape to the underside of the flap and the hook portion to a corresponding point on the case front. Sew a decorative button to the flap, covering the stitching line of the hook-and-loop tape. Set the case aside.

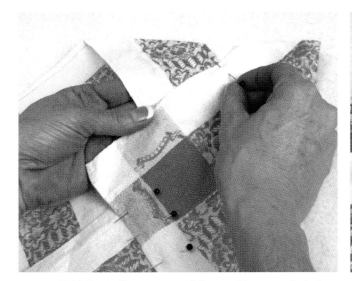

STEP 1 Fold the bottom corner of the napkin up and pin in place.

STEP 4 Secure the envelope flap with hook-and-loop tape.

5. To make the pillow insert for the envelope case, use a pinking blade or scissors to cut a square or rectangle pillow front and back, slightly smaller than the case. Cut a small rectangle, 2½ in. by 3 in., for the pocket. Cut a piece of hook-and-loop tape ½ in. by 1 in.

6. Sew the loop portion of the tape to the inside of the pocket, centered and ⅜ in. from the top. Sew the hook portion of the tape on the pillow front, centered and ⅝ in. from the top. Lay the pocket on top of the pillow front, aligning the hook and loop tape, and stitch in place, ¼ in. from the edge, leaving the top open.

7. Place the pillow front and back wrong sides together. Stitch around the pillow edge, using a ¼-in. to ½-in. seam allowance, leaving one side open. Through the open end, lightly fill the pillow with quilt batting or polyester stuffing. Topstitch the remain-

The small pocket on the front of the pillow insert will hold the tooth or money.

ing side closed. Insert the pillow in the envelope case and you're ready for the tooth fairy!

Here are some other creative ideas for small pillows:

✦ Make a larger version of the tooth-fairy pillow and as your child grows, put special written messages into the pocket.
✦ Make a similar pillow to hold the rings during a wedding ceremony.
✦ Make the pillow and pocket large enough to hold a special gift, like jewelry, or a small doll.

CHAPTER SIX

VINTAGE TEXTILES IN HOME DECOR

I t's time to pull out those vintage textiles you've been collecting, or purchase a few of the pieces you've been admiring, and begin recycling and restyling to transform the charms of the past into contemporary items for your home. Combine beautiful, old fabrics, laces, linens, buttons, and trims with new textiles and home furnishings in a way that fits your lifestyle. Take the ideas and techniques we've applied to clothing and put them to use in your home.

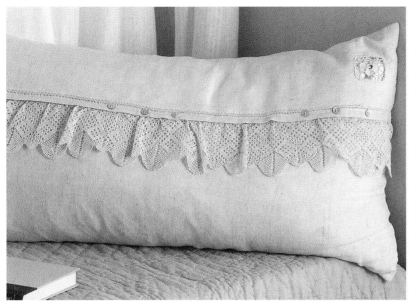

Combine vintage elements to create pretty pillows, like this one from lace, buttons, and a cutwork tablecloth.

To make this pillow, I folded a square tablecloth wrong sides together and topstitched along the three edges, next to the pink crocheted edge.

PILLOWS

Pillows add character and charm to your decor and provide you with an opportunity to sew creatively, whether you are an advanced sewer or a beginner. Tablecloths, napkins, embroidered or beaded dresser scarves and towels, quilts and quilt tops, vintage fabrics; just about any vintage textile can be used to make a pillow. Combine familiar construction methods with techniques from chapter 4 and keep the design of the pillow simple to highlight the textile. Pillows composed of vintage fabric offer endless creative possibilities—here are just a few.

Make a Fold, Create a Pillow

It is not uncommon to find small, square tablecloths embellished with embroidery, cutwork, or lace that can be folded over to create a rectangular pillow. In the example above left, I wanted to leave the tablecloth and lace intact without cutting into either vintage piece. Follow these steps to create this style pillow:

This pink pillow was made from a rectangular cotton towel that was stitched with embroidery on both ends.

MATERIALS
+ *Small square or rectangular tablecloth*
+ *Lace edging*
+ *Small buttons*
+ *White fabric for pillow form*
+ *Polyester stuffing*

1. Gather the plain edge of the lace to fit one edge of the tablecloth. Spread out the tablecloth right side up on your worktable. Place the lace right side up on top of it, aligning the gathered edge with one edge of the cloth, and baste (see the top illustration at right).

2. Turn the cloth wrong side up. Fold up the edge with the lace. Fold up the opposite edge and overlap it on the lace by about ½ in. Pin the overlap together, making a tube (slip your hand underneath so you don't pin through to the rest of the tablecloth). Sew the overlapped layers together. Add small buttons (see the bottom illustration at right).

3. Lay the tube flat on your worktable, and rotate the layers until the lace ruffle sits in an attractive position. Mark the top fold with a pin at each end of the tube. Turn the tube wrong side out, and lay it flat on your worktable so it folds at the pin marks. Pin the layers together at one end of the tube. Sew, using a ½-in. seam allowance. Turn the pillow cover right side out and lay it flat on your worktable.

4. Measure the pillow cover and subtract ½ in. from the length (for the seam across the open end). Mark two rectangles this size on the white fabric, adding seam allowance all around. Cut them out. Sew together along three edges. Fill with stuffing. Fold in and sew the fourth edge closed. Insert the pillow into the pillow cover. Fold in the open edge of the cover, and hand-sew it closed.

Sew a Seam, Tie an End

Make decorative bolster pillows to complement your sofa or bed, using large tea towels or dish towels embellished with lace and embroidery.

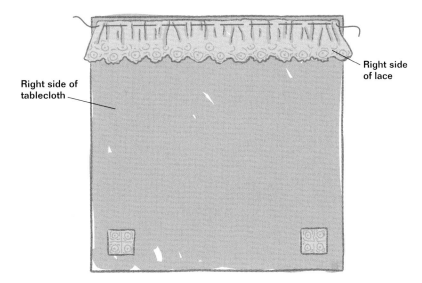

Wrong side of lace to right side of tablecloth

Right side of tablecloth

Right side of lace

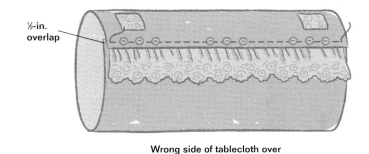

½-in. overlap

Wrong side of tablecloth over right side of the lace

A Victorian towel was used to make this small bolster pillow.

STEP 1 **A placement line for the ribbon casing is marked equidistant from each end of the towel.**

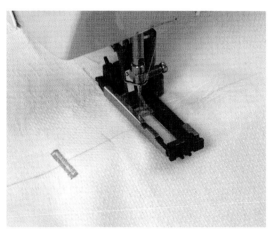

STEP 2 **Two buttonholes are placed over the placement line on each end to allow the ribbon to be threaded through the casing.**

STEP 4 **Sew the twill tape down over the placement line, using an edgestitch foot.**

+ *Embroidered damask or linen towel*
+ *Small bolster pillow or quilt batting*
+ *2 yd. ¾-in.-wide ribbon*
+ *1-in.-wide twill tape*

1. Wrap the linen towel around the bolster and loosely gather each end to determine the placement of the end ribbons; measure this distance from the towel end. (If you are using quilt batting, roll it up to make a small bolster shape.) With a chalk marker, mark a placement line on the wrong side of the towel, parallel to and this distance from each end. Mark the midpoint of each line.

2. On each end of the towel, make two 1-in.-long buttonholes, each 1 in. from the midpoint marking and perpendicular to the towel end. Open the buttonholes.

3. Fold the towel in half lengthwise, wrong side out. Using a ½-in. seam allowance, sew the long edges together to make a tube. Press open the seam.

4. To make a casing for each tie, center a length of twill tape over the marked placement line at each end of the towel, overlapping the twill tape ends. Use an edgestitch foot to sew each edge of the tape to the towel.

5. Turn the tube right side out. Cut the ribbon into two 1-yd. pieces. With a safety pin or bodkin, thread one piece through each casing, inserting it through one buttonhole and bringing it out through the other.

6. Insert the pillow or quilt batting into the pillow cover, draw the ribbons up tightly, and tie them into bows. The pillow cover can be further embellished with buttons, ribbons, and laces.

Common background fabric used to make these pillows helps unify the variety of dresser scarves and hand towels that embellishes the pillow tops.

Combine Textiles

Expand the creative possibilities and make the most of the available fabric by making a pillow from a combination of vintage textiles. In the examples above, embroidered dresser scarves and hand towels were cut to the desired size and sewn into the seam at the top of the pillow. The vintage piece was secured to the pillow front with vintage buttons and ribbon embellishment. The pillow forms were inserted through button-closed overlapped openings in the back.

Showcase the beauty of the vintage doilies, embroidered pieces, ribbons, beads, and buttons by layering them on top of contrasting fabric. Make a whole grouping of "period piece" pillows by simply sewing vintage handkerchiefs to pillow tops before construction. The pillow embellishments shown at right and in the top photo on p. 116 were sewn to the pillow top before construction.

Can't fall asleep? Study the state maps on these vintage handkerchief pillows and dream away.

Layer favorite doilies, laces, embroidered pieces, and buttons and trims over a background fabric before constructing the pillow top.

Here, a vintage needlepoint was applied to a wool melton pillow top using the reverse appliqué technique.

Add Lace

The beauty and abundance of vintage lace creates endless possibilities for pillow design. Each piece of lace is unique in the way it was constructed and the materials used, as well as in its length, width, and color. Use the lace as the focus of the design, or apply it more subtly to create texture and dimension. Use tone-on-tone color combinations by adding white- or cream-colored lace to the same- or similar-colored linens. Sew lace to linens embellished with bright embroidery or appliqué. Add lace to patterned vintage fabrics, or dye the lace to the color you want. Experiment to find the least conspicuous and simplest way to attach the lace.

The pillow shown in the top photo on the facing page was made from a combination of a vintage dresser scarf, new fabric, and lace edging removed from two worn pillowcases. For the pillow front and back, two pieces of new fabric were cut slightly longer than the rectangular, embroidered dresser scarf, and their width equaled half the circumference of the lace edging (plus ½ in. for seam allowance all around). The dresser scarf was centered and topstitched to the right side of one of the pieces of background fabric. A square pearl button was sewn to the pillow center and a Victorian, hand-painted shoe button was

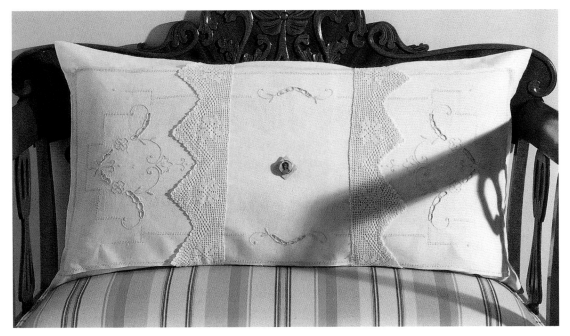

I combined a pretty dresser scarf and the lace borders from two pillowcases to make this rectangular pillow.

glued to the pearl button. With right sides together, the pillow front and back were sewn together on the two long sides and across one end, turned right sides out and pressed. A pillow form was inserted into the pillowcase, and the remaining end was slipstitched closed. The pieces of lace were slipped onto the pillow, positioned over the dresser scarf, and hand-stitched in place.

Nightgown Bag Pillow

Visiting antiques stores in England I discovered fabric bags embellished with beautiful laces labeled "nightgown bags," which were meant to store these garments neatly out of sight. The design is similar to an envelope. One end of a rectangular piece of fabric is folded up to create a pocket for the nightgown, and the other end is folded over to create a flap. Embellished with a button and ribbon and filled with a folded gown or a pillow insert, the nightgown bag makes a beautiful pillow. If you like, add decorative stitches, corded pintucks, stenciling, or stamping to the fabric before cutting it out.

MATERIALS

✦ *½ yd. fabric for pillow*
✦ *18-in. pillow*
✦ *Ribbons, buttons, cording, beads, etc.*

To create this simple nightgown-bag pillow:

1. Cut a rectangular piece of fabric 18 in. wide and 36 in. long (adjust these measure-

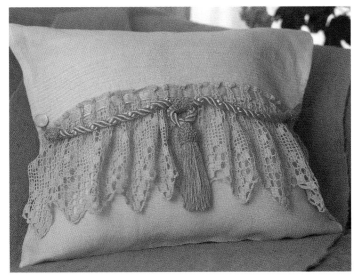

Corded pintucks and lace were added to the flap of this pillow. The vintage drapery tieback buttons at the flap edges.

Nightgown Bag Pillow

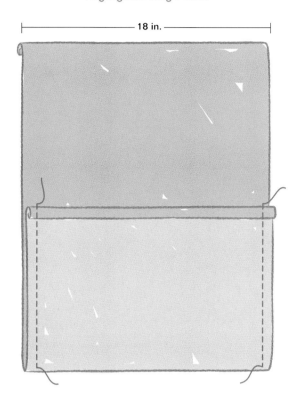

|← 18 in. →|

ments to accommodate the vintage textiles you are using).

2. Form a hem along the 18-in. edges by pressing under ¼ in., then ½ in. on each and stitching. Place the fabric right side up on your worktable and fold up 12 in. at one 18-in. end. Pin and sew the fabric layers together along each edge, using a ½-in. seam allowance. Hem the edges of the flap by hand and turn the pocket right side out.

3. Embellish the flap with laces, ribbons, cording, buttons, beads, etc.

Recycle a Sweater or Scarf

Create cozy accessories from old wool sweaters, jackets, and scarves. Take that hand-knitted sweater you've held onto for years or the scarf that's been outdated since you acquired it, and create an inviting pillow. Cut garments apart first and finish the edges to prevent unraveling, then wash and dry them to create more texture and dimension.

Vintage needle-point pieces are readily available and can make a dramatic statement when used to make pillow tops.

Old sweaters and jackets make whimsical or tailored modern pillows.

Incorporate features like pockets and buttons or the fringe of a scarf into your pillow design, combine them with other fabrics and embellish with buttons, trims, and wool yarns.

Duvet Cover: A Large Pillow Sham

Duvets have enjoyed a comeback recently, and what better way to recall their history than by using vintage fabrics for their covers. A duvet cover is essentially a giant pillow sham. I love them for combining the look of an earlier time with the practicality of modern life. My favorite is made from a vintage damask tablecloth and natural, medium-weight linen, and closed with large, mismatched, old buttons.

Though large pieces of fabric must be handled, making a duvet cover is a simple project. Use a tablecloth and fabric combination that is lightweight for maximum warmth with minimal weight. The cover can be embellished with vintage trims and laces, layered with embroidered pieces, or left unadorned.

In my design I wanted to contrast the shiny, white tablecloth with the rougher-textured natural linen. I used a white damask tablecloth for the front, and ecru linen for the back and for a 15-in.-deep band along one edge of the front—you can see this band running along the side of the bed in the bottom photo on p. 121. This band provides the envelope-style opening on the front; I call it the "envelope band." It is actually cut in one piece with the back and folded over to the front, but you can cut it separately and sew it to the duvet back if you like.

The following material requirements are for a 50-in. by 72-in. duvet cover, which will easily contain a 48-in. by 70-in. comforter. I turn this comforter sideways on a queen-size bed, which is why the linen strip runs lengthwise in the photograph. Read the directions all the way through before beginning, because, depending upon the size of your tablecloth and comforter, you may have to adjust the order of the planning steps. You'll probably find it helpful to make a schematic draw-

To create a pillow form, cut two pieces of lightweight cotton or polyester fabric, adding ½ in. around for seam allowances. With right sides together, sew around, leaving a 6-in. space on one side. Turn the pillow right side out, stuff, and slipstitch the opening closed.

ing showing the dimensions to help you figure out how large to cut each piece.

MATERIALS:

- ✦ *Comforter: 48 in. by 70 in.*
- ✦ *3 yd. 60-in.-wide fabric for back*
- ✦ *Tablecloth*
- ✦ *Extra fabric to increase measurement of tablecloth, if needed*

TRY THIS

✦ Use the same idea for the duvet cover and cover a large rectangular bed pillow. In the example above, a Victorian towel was centered over the front, with stacked vintage buttons added for embellishment. The pillow is inserted through an overlapped opening in the back.

✦ Piece together a duvet top. Use vintage handkerchiefs, embroidered dresser scarves, recycled wool suiting fabrics, and other vintage textiles.

✦ Topstitch a colorful '50s style tablecloth, a lace tablecloth, or an embroidered tablecloth to a background fabric and use it for the duvet top. Place it diagonally on the background fabric if you like.

✦ Use vintage fabric to cover large buttons for an interesting closure.

- ✦ *¼ yd. lightweight fusible interfacing*
- ✦ *¼ yd. medium-weight fusible interfacing*
- ✦ *Five or more large buttons*

1. Measure the width and length of the comforter. Add 2 in. to each dimension for ease.

2. Measure the usable area of your tablecloth. If one of the dimensions is not at least as long as one of the comforter dimensions, you'll have to piece another fabric onto it to make it equal, so plan for how you'll do that. If the tablecloth is larger than the comforter dimensions, decide how you'll cut it down—if it has a centered or symmetrical pattern, you'll want to trim equally from opposite edges. Remember there will be an envelope band along one edge of the cover—this band can be almost any depth, so while it can compensate for a skimpy tablecloth, it can also force you to cut a cloth that is large. Be sure to allow for an overlap (or underlap) where the envelope band meets the tablecloth. You'll need seam allowances all around, including a deep hem allowance to support the buttons.

3. According to your tablecloth calculations, you should next decide how deep the envelope band should be and which edge of the comforter you want to put it on. Add the dimensions of the band to the appropriate edge of the back. Add seam allowances all around, including a deep hem allowance along the edge of the band to support the buttonholes.

4. Double-check all your calculations. Measure and mark the dimensions on the tablecloth and fabric, and cut out the pieces.

5. Next, reinforce the overlapping area of the envelope band and tablecloth with interfacing. I used lightweight fusible interfacing for the tablecloth because it kept the soft hand

of the damask. I used a medium-weight fusible interfacing for the linen.

6. Hem the interfaced edge of the tablecloth and of the linen.

7. To create the envelope band, place the linen right side up on your worktable, with the hemmed edge toward you. From the hem edge, measure the chosen depth of the envelope band, and fold the linen back this amount all across (see the photo at right). Pin the layers together at each end. Place the tablecloth right side down on top of the linen, aligning the cut edges and overlapping the hems. Pin all around. Sew all around, using whatever seam allowance you planned.

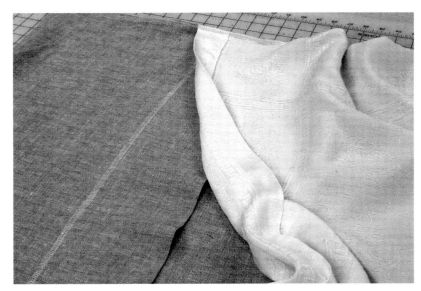

The top of the duvet front (the white tablecloth in my example) is layered over the fold in the duvet back (the linen) to create the envelope-style opening.

Vintage linens combined with the right fabric make a restful bed ensemble.

8. Turn the duvet cover right side out and press. Measure and mark evenly spaced buttonholes on the linen hem (I used five), then make the buttonholes. Sew buttons on the tablecloth hem to correspond to the buttonholes.

SLIPCOVERS

Slipcovers let you change the look of a piece of furniture or an entire room with the addition of fabric. Whether you use slipcovers to protect furniture, cover tattered upholstery, change the mood of a room, or hide that horrid piece your in-laws gave you, a little bit of effort and sewing finesse can go a long way. Don't let the idea of making slipcovers intimidate you. If you can wrap a present, you can make the following simple slipcovers.

Dining-Room Chairs Turn Their Backs

When you step into a dining room, typically the chairs are pushed in to the table, and what you see is the back of the chair. Make your view interesting by adding a slipcover to the chair back and incorporating vintage tablecloths, handkerchiefs, embroidered dresser scarves, lace, buttons, and anything else that appeals to you.

For the slipcover in the left photo on the facing page, I cut two rectangular pieces of fabric—one for the slipcover front and one for the back. When I sewed the seam that would go across the top of the chair back, I inserted the corner of a vintage tablecloth. Then I placed the joined rectangles on the chair and wrapped them over the sides, tucking in the excess along the sides, as though I were wrapping a package. I used buttons and buttonholes to secure the sides at the bottom. Here are general instructions for these simply designed and constructed slipcovers. Your chairs, vintage textiles, and design will differ

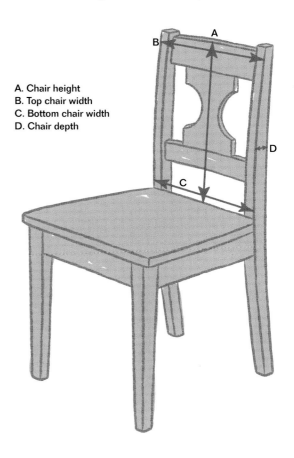

A. Chair height
B. Top chair width
C. Bottom chair width
D. Chair depth

from mine, so adjust accordingly. Before beginning, launder the materials so there won't be any surprise shrinkage after the slipcovers are finished.

MATERIALS
+ *⅔ yd. fabric for each slipcover*
+ *Masking tape*
+ *Vintage textiles*
+ *Interfacing*
+ *Buttons*

1. Make a schematic drawing of your chair back. Measure the chair back, and jot the following measurements on the drawing: Height, width at top, width at seat, depth from back to front (thickness) (see the illustration above).

If you want to make multiples of a slipcover, make paper or muslin patterns from the cover you have measured and pin-fitted. Mark all seamlines, seam allowances, buttonhole markings, and placement marks on the new pattern to save time and improve accuracy.

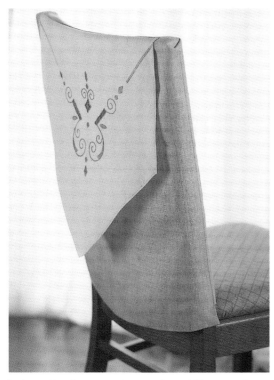

A simple button closure allows the slipcover to slip on the chair easily.

It doesn't take extensive sewing skills to make these simple chair-back slipcovers.

2. These covers are so easy to fit that you don't really have to make a pattern. Just cut two slightly oversized rectangles from your fabric, making the length equal to the height of the chair back plus generous seam and hem allowances, and the width equal to the greater chair back width-plus-depth plus generous side-hem allowances.

3. Pin or baste the rectangles together along the top seam, and place them over the chair back. Fold the bottom of each rectangle up at seat level; pin. Fold the sides of the front rectangle toward the back; tape temporarily to the chair. Fold the sides of the back rectangle toward the front; pin in place. Mark the front edge of the chair on each side with pins or chalk. Unpin the back, and on the front rectangle piece, mark the back edge of the chair with pins or chalk. Identify the front and back rectangles with chalk marks in case they are not the same.

4. Lift the fabric off the chair. Use chalk to mark the fold on the pinned lower edges; unpin. Next use chalk and a ruler to straighten all the marked lines, then mark and rule a hem allowance on the bottoms and side edges, and a seam allowance on the top edges. Cut out the pieces along the outer marked lines. Finish the edges if you wish.

5. Cut the vintage textile to fit the back of the chair in a way you like, hemming any cut edges that won't be caught in the seam at the top of the slipcover. To use the tablecloth corner, I first cut off a triangular piece 22 in. from the corner point, then trimmed the excess width, as shown in the left illustration on p. 124.

6. Place the slipcover back piece right side up on your worktable. Lay the vintage piece right side up on top of it, aligning the top edges. Place the front slipcover right side

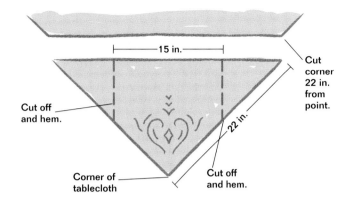

15 in.

Cut off
and hem.

Cut
corner
22 in.
from
point.

22 in.

Corner of
tablecloth

Cut off
and hem.

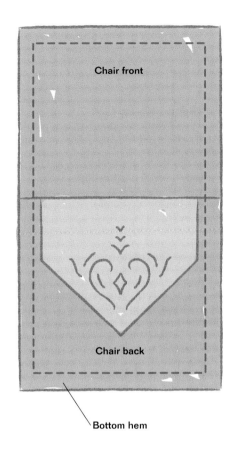

Chair front

Chair back

Bottom hem

down on top of the vintage linen. Pin and sew
the top seam. Press the seam allowance open.

7. Cut out and then fuse the interfacing to
the hem allowances all around the slipcover.
Fold up and press the hems all around, miter-
ing the corners or folding them neatly.

8. Place the slipcover on the chair. Wrap the
front toward the back, and tape in place temporarily again. Wrap the back toward the front
and pin securely. Lift the slipcover off the
chair. Topstitch the back to the front on both
sides, stopping about halfway down on one
side. In the hem on the open edge of the back,
mark and sew two evenly spaced buttonholes.

9. Sew corresponding buttons to the front
(see the right photo on p. 123).

Slipcover a Side Table

Combine vintage textiles to make a cover for a
side table. In this example two well-worn
tablecloths were used to make a floor-length
cover for an inexpensive round table. Use
cotton or polyester as the underlining fabric,
or use quilt batting if you want the tabletop to
have a soft appearance.

MATERIALS
+ *Tracing paper or muslin*
+ *Vintage tablecloths or fabric*
+ *Underlining fabric*
+ *Covered button kit or vintage buttons*

1. Lay a piece of muslin or tracing paper
over the tabletop, and trace the outline. Add
½-in. seam allowances around the tracing, and
cut out the pattern. From the pattern, cut out
one piece from your vintage fabric and one
from the underlining fabric. Lay the vintage
fabric wrong side up on your worktable. Lay
the underlining on top of it. Baste the two
fabrics together.

2. To determine the width of the skirt, first measure the perimeter of the tabletop. Add to this an allowance for four inverted box pleats, planning them to be whatever depth you'd like. This measurement gives you the finished width of the skirt; you'll need a seam allowance for at least one seam and probably more, depending upon your fabric. To determine the length of the skirt, measure from the tabletop to the floor; add a ½-in. seam allowance plus whatever hem allowance you'd like.

3. For the skirt in the photo at right, I cut a rectangular vintage tablecloth in half lengthwise and sewed the ends together to make a piece long enough to go around the table and fold into pleats. Referring to the measurements taken in step 2, plan how to cut the skirt from your fabric. Cut out the pieces and

Create a beautiful tablecloth for an inexpensive table by combining vintage linens.

⁀ TRY THIS

+ Combine vintage laces, dresser scarves, or embroidered tablecloths with new fabrics.

+ Change the skirt design to a gathered skirt.

+ For a tailored look, add a button placket to one or more sides of the skirt.

+ To create a pretty overlay for the table skirt, sew vintage handkerchiefs side by side onto a length of bias or twill tape. Then insert the tape in the seam between the cover top and skirt.

+ Make a cover for a circular or rectangular

Make a cover for a trunk or chest, incorporating inverted box pleats at each corner. Add a button placket detail down each side.

footstool or ottoman, using the same principle. It will work to cover a trunk as well—try using a vintage camp blanket for a rustic look.

Slipcover for a Round Table

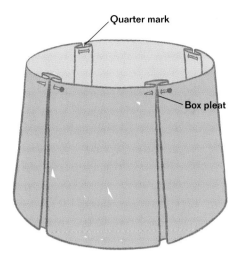

Quarter mark

Box pleat

sew them together so they form a large tube. Hem the bottom edge of the tube.

4. Divide the perimeter of the tabletop fabric into fourths and mark. Divide the top edge of the skirt tube into fourths and mark (if your table is square or rectangular, divide and mark the skirt for a pleat at each corner). Fold an inverted box pleat into the skirt fabric at each mark, and pin in place (see the illustration at left).

5. With right sides together and cut edges aligned, pin the skirt to the tabletop fabric, matching a pleat to each mark (put the pins in along the seamline, not across it). Put the table cover on the table wrong side up, and check the fit; if it doesn't hang well, adjust it by increasing or decreasing the pleat depth all around. Place the pinned fabrics on the sewing machine with the tabletop fabric on top; sew the tabletop to the skirt. Finish the seam-allowance edges.

6. Using a button-covering kit and following the manufacturer's directions, cover four buttons and sew one to the skirt at the top of each pleat.

If you look closely, you will see less-than-perfect stitches on this valance, but what is appreciated is the delicate design and color.

WINDOW TREATMENTS

Vintage textiles can be used to make window treatments as long as you consider the physical characteristics of the window and the condition of the vintage pieces. If the fabric has serious stains or damage, or if the piece has significant sentimental value, you probably won't want to risk hanging it in your window. Direct sunlight can damage fabrics quickly, particularly vulnerable vintage fabrics. If a textile is weak or delicate, it may not withstand the effects of gravity. And if a window is large or if a room has many windows, most vintage textiles will be too small; but consider this an opportunity for combining textiles.

Having said all this, however, sometimes it seems such a waste to keep beautiful linens and laces tucked away in a drawer or box. Why not make a beautiful vintage embroidered tablecloth into a valance, or drape a knitted lace tablecloth over a window for a light and airy window treatment? Bring your sense of ingenuity and inventiveness to the table as you work vintage textiles into window-treatment designs. Mix old textiles with new—just try to avoid direct sunlight. Consider the ideas that follow.

TRY THIS

✦ Stitch or appliqué vintage textiles to new fabric to make window treatments. This allows you to take advantage of small or damaged pieces. Additionally, the supporting fabric will protect fragile textiles from adverse exposure to the sun. In the photo at right, you can see I used the scraps from my dining-chair slipcovers to embellish the window treatments. Handkerchiefs and elegant silk scarves are some other choices.

✦ Stitch lace to the bottom or top of a window treatment, or attach it to a curtain tieback.

✦ Drape vintage tablecloths over a curtain rod or between hooks for a simple window treatment.

Embroidered areas from a tablecloth were appliquéd to the tops of these curtains.

✦ Sew lace to the hem of a tablecloth and fold, swag, or clip it over a curtain rod.

✦ Layer vintage napkins placed on the diagonal over a curtain rod for a short valance.

The design of birds on the embroidered dresser scarf used for this valance fit the theme of the room.

Embellished Valance

Give a simple tab valance more interest by adding a vintage dresser scarf. I designed the valance shown above to hang quite flatly, without gathers, so the embroidery on the dresser scarf could be appreciated. Modify the following instructions to suit your window and fabric—just keep the dimensions of your dresser scarf in mind as you plan the size of the valance. Install the curtain rod before measuring so you'll be able to plan accurately.

MATERIALS

- *Fabric for tab valance*
- *Vintage dresser scarf, shorter in length and width than valance*
- *Rod for valance*
- *Two hooks or other method to attach curtain rod to wall*

1. Determine the width of the valance by measuring the width of the window and adding a side-hem allowance plus 5 in. to 10 in. for a little ease. Decide how deep you want the valance to be, add a bottom-hem

allowance and a top-seam allowance. Cut the valance to these measurements. Also cut a facing the same width as the valance but only 3 in. deep.

2. To form the tabs that go over the rod, cut the desired number of tabs twice as wide as needed, plus seam allowance, and long enough to go over the rod, plus seam allowance. The finished length of the valance is 12 in. and the finished size of the tabs is 3 in. by 6 in.

3. Hem the sides and bottom of the valance. Hem only the bottom of the facing. Fold each tab in half lengthwise, right sides together. Sew each long edge, then turn right side out. Press with the seam centered down the back.

4. Place the valance right side up on your worktable. Center the dresser scarf on top of it, right side up, aligning the top edges. Baste in place.

5. Turn the valance wrong side up. Fold the tabs in half, cut edges even, seamed side in. Evenly space the folded tabs across the top edge of the valance, aligning the cut edges, and baste in place.

6. Place the facing, right side down, on top of the wrong side of the valance, aligning the cut edges. Pin and sew together along the top edge. Fold the facing over to the right side of the valance, extending the tabs above the fold. Pin and press. Fold the ends of the facing under, even with the sides of the valance. Topstitch the lower edge of the facing to the valance.

STEP 5 **Place the folded tab against the wrong side of the valance.**

STEP 6 **Topstitch the lower edge of the facing to the valance.**

HANGING ORGANIZER

Use vintage fabrics to create this hanging organizer to hold shoes, stuffed animals, and other treasures. I unified a white damask tablecloth, lace, and a piece of fabric left over from a previous project by dyeing them pink, and cut the binding from old flour sacks. You can easily create your own version. If you want to add trim, you'll need enough to go across the bottom of each row of pockets. To keep the top edge of the organizer stiff, sew a casing to the back to hold a dowel; be sure the dowel is a couple of inches shorter than the organizer width. The finished size of the organizer shown is 18 in. by 33 in., with three rows of three pleated pockets, each pocket 6 in. wide by 6½ in. deep.

To hang this pocket organizer, simply slip the strap over two over-the-door plastic hooks.

MATERIALS

+ 2¼ yd. fabric for organizer front, back, pockets, and cord covering
+ ¼ yd. pocket binding
+ ¾ yd. flannel or quilt batting
+ 1⅔ yd. lace or trim
+ 2 yd. cord for hanging loop
+ one 16-in.-long dowel, ⅜ in. in diameter

1. For the back of the organizer, cut two pieces 19 in. by 34 in. from your fabric; cut one piece the same size from flannel or batting. For the pockets, cut three pieces of fabric 13 in. by 31 in. Cut three crosswise or bias strips for the pocket edge bindings, each 2⅝ in. by 31 in. Cut a 2-in. by 36-in. bias strip to cover the hanging cord. Cut a 1¾-in. by 16-in. strip for the dowel casing.

2. Finish the edge of the dowel casing. Pin it to the organizer back, 1 in. below the top end and centered between the sides. Topstitch in place.

3. Place the two back pieces right sides together on your worktable. Place the flannel on top. Using a ½-in. seam allowance, sew together around the edges, leaving an opening in one side. Trim corners. Slip your hand between the fabric layers and turn the back right side out. Press. Slipstitch the opening closed.

4. Fold the pocket strips in half lengthwise, wrong sides together. Press, then baste the cut edges together. Bind the long cut edge of each pocket strip, using a ⅝-in. seam allowance and the method described in chapter 3, Binding an Edge.

RESOURCES

Sewing Supplies

Ah! Kimono
16004 NE 195th St.
Woodinville, WA 98072-6459
(425) 482-6485
ginko@ahkimono.com
kimono and coordinated kimono sample packs

Banasch's
2810 Highland Ave.
Cincinnati, OH 45212
(800) 543-0355
www.banaschs.com
stain-removal products

Beadcats
Carol Perrenoud & Virginia Blakelock
Universal Synergistics Inc. Bead Store
P.O. Box 2840
Wilsonville, OR 97070-2840
(503) 625-2323
(503) 625-4329 FAX
www.beadcats.com
beads, beading supplies

Clotilde Inc.
B3000
Louisiana MO 63353-3000
(800) 772-2891
www.clotilde.com
*notions, including iron cleaners,
detergents for fabrics; catalog*

Design and Sew Patterns
Lois Ericson
P.O. Box 5222
Salem, OR 97304
patterns

Dharma Trading Co.
Box 150916
San Rafael, CA 94915
(800) 542-5227
www.dharmatrading.com
fabric paints, dyes; catalog

Hot Potatoes
2805 Columbine Pl.
Nashville, TN 37204
(615) 269-8002
www.hotpotatoes.com
fabric stamps; catalog

Nancy's Notions
P.O. Box 583
Beaver Dam, WI 53916-0683
(800) 833-0690
www.nancynotions.com
*notions, including fabric stabilizers, iron
cleaners, detergents for fabrics*

Proctor and Gamble Co.
P.O. Box 599
Cincinnati, Ohio 45212
(800) 214-8913
www.dryel.com
home dry-cleaning product

Revisions/Diane Ericson
Box 7404
Carmel, CA 93921
stencils and books; catalog

SF Designs
1234 Spruance St.
San Jose, CA 95128
(408) 971-1767
patterns

The Sewing Workshop Collection
2010 Balboa St.
San Francisco, CA 94121
(415) 221-7397
(800) 466-1599
www.sewingworkshop.com
pattern, books

The Soap and Detergent Assoc.
1500 K St. NW, Suite 300
Washington, DC 20005
(202) 347-2900
www.sdahq.org

Things Japanese
9805 N.E. 116th, Suite 7160
Kirkland, WA 98034-4248
(206) 821-2287
metallic fabric paint, silk thread; catalog

Threadwear
1250 S.W. Oakley Ave.
Topeka, Kansas 66604
(785) 235-1552
www.sewingworkshop.com
fabrics, patterns, books

Yarn Barn
930 Massachusetts
Lawrence, KS 66044
(800) 468-0035
(785) 842-4333
www.yarnbarn-ks.com
fabric dyes, wool-melton mill ends, books, videos

Yesterday and Today
Terri LaForge
4 Roberts Block
Glenside, PA 19038
(215) 572-6926
vintageangel247@aol.com
vintage buttons, handwork, fabrics

Books

Fine Embellishment Techniques
by Jane Conlon
The Taunton Press
63 South Main St.
Newtown, CT 06470
This book discusses a variety of beading techniques.

Simply Slipcovers
Sunset Books, Inc.,
Menlo, Park, CA 94025
This book discusses construction techniques for home-decorating projects.

Flea Market Style, Decorating with a Creative Edge
by Emelie Tolley and Chris Mead
Clarkson N. Potter, Inc.
201 East 50th St.
New York, NY 10022
This book discusses choosing and decorating with flea-market finds and includes a directory of flea markets around the country.

Sewing Luxurious Pillows: Artistic Designs for Home Decor
by Linda Lee
Sterling Publishing Company, Inc.
387 Park Ave. S.
New York, NY 10016

Art Deco Cut and Use Stencils
by Theodore Menten
Dover Publications, Inc.
31 East 2nd St.
Mineola, NY 11501

Art Deco Designs in Color
by Charles Rahn Fry
Dover Publications, Inc.
31 East 2nd St.
Mineola, NY 11501

Index

L

Lace, 9
    adding length to garment with, *38*, 43-44, *44*
    adding to pillows, 116, *116*, 117, *117*
    embellishing with, 60-61, *61*, 62, *62*, 63, *63*
    preventing unraveling, 45, *45*
    removing, 61, *61*, 62, *62*
Laundering, tolerance of, 10
Linen/linens, 6, 8, *8*, 24

M

Mildew, 12, 16
Moth/insect damage, 10

N

Napkins, 9
Needle and stitch length, 32
Needlepoint, 6, 9, *24*
    blocking vintage needlepoint, 66
    pieces for purses, *71*
    pillow tops, *118*
    in reverse appliqué, 65, *65*, 66, *66*, 67, *67*, 68
"Nightgown bags," 117-18, **118**

P

Pattern layout, developing:
    adding a yoke, 40, *40*, 41
    adding length with lace, *38*, 43-44, *44*
    binding an edge, 41, *41*, 42, *42*
    combining fabrics, 44, 46, *46*, 48-49, *49*
    copying an original pattern, 38, *38*, 49
    cutting out, 49-50, *50*
    dividing pattern pieces, 39, *39*, 40, *40*
    example of vintage piece(s) to completed garment, 46-50
    fabric shortage options, 38-46
    laying out a pattern, 49, *49*
    making bias binding, 41-42, *42*
    making a self-faced sleeve cuff, 51, *51*
    modifying a pattern, 39-44, 47-48, *48*
    neckline finish as a design feature, 43, *43*
    selecting a pattern, 28-29, *29*, 30, 47, *47*
    shortening pattern pieces, 39, *39*
    two-piece sleeves, 40, *40*
Pattern selection, 28-29, 30
    design detail of pattern, to complement vintage textile, 30
    personal style and, 28-29
Perspiration damage, 11, 14, 15
Piecing vintage textiles, 56, *56*, 57
Pillows:
    adding lace, 116, *116*, 117, *117*
    bolster pillows, 113, *113*, 114, *114*
    combining textiles, 115, *115*, 116
    folding and creating a pillow, 112, *112*, 113, **113**
    "nightgown bags," 117-18, **118**
    recycling a sweater or scarf, 118-19, *119*
    with sheer cover, 56-57, *57*, 58
    tooth-fairy pillow, 108, *108*, 109, *109*
Pintuck embellishment, 73, *73*
Potpourri bags, 20, *20*, 21, *21*
Pressing:
    equipment and special handling, 19, *19*
    linens, 18
Projects:
    Christmas stockings, 52, *52*, 53, *53*
    designer gift bags, 34, *34*, 35, *35*
    hanging organizer, 130, *130*, 131, *131*
    potpourri bags, 20, *20*, 21, *21*
    tooth-fairy pillow, 108, *108*, 109, *109*
    vintage purses, 86, *86*, 87, *87*
Purses, 9, *71*, 86, *86*, 87, *87*

Q

Quilts/quilt pieces/quilt blocks, 9
Quilt top, *57*

R

Reverse appliqué, 65, *65*, 66, *66*, 67, *67*, 68, *102*, 116

S

Scarves, *6*, 8, *68*, 69, *115*
Seam finishes, 32
Sewing:
    buttonholes, 33, *33*
    interfacing, 26, 31-32
    making samples, 33, *33*
    needle, stitch length, and thread, 32-33
    sequence modifications, 31, *32*
Sheer overlay, 56-57, *57*, 58
Side table slipcovers, 124-25, *125*, 126, **126**
Silk vintage pieces, 11
Sleeves:
    making a self-faced sleeve cuff, 51, *51*
    shortened, 39, *39*
    two-piece, 40, *40*
Slipcovers:
    chairs, 122, **122**, 123, *123*, 124, **124**
    side table, 124-25, *125*, 126, **126**
Stain removal:
    acid-based stains, 14
    identifying stains, *10*, 14
    iron/rust stains, 14, 15-16
    methods in antique cookbooks/diaries, 13-14, *14*
    mildew, 16
    oil-based stains, 14, 15
    overall whitening and deodorizing, 16, *16*
    perspiration stains, 14, 15
    protein stains, 14, 15, *15*
    treating stains, 14-15, *15*, 16
    using bleach, 15, 16
    water-based stains, 14
Stamping vintage fabric, 76-77, *77*
Stenciling vintage fabric, 74, *74*, 75, *75*, 76, *76*
Sweaters, 8, 118-19, *119*

T

Tablecloths, turning into clothing, *7*, 8, *26*, 46-50, 100, *100*
Tea dyeing, 17
Thread, 32-33
Ties, 8, 9
Tooth-fairy pillow, 108, *108*, 109, *109*
Towels, hand and kitchen, 8

W

Window treatments, 127, *127*, 128, *128*, 129, *129*
Workmanship of textile and material, 9
Worn areas, 10